D0913686

1. Ice Bean
   (Soy Ice Cream)
2. Soybeans
3. Tempeh
4. Tofu
5. Soybean Burrito
6. Tofu Cheesecake
7. Soymilk

PUBLISHER: Paul Mandelstein

EDITOR: Louise Hagler

CONTRIBUTING EDITORS: Janet Mundo, Laurie Praskin, Cynthia Bates, Anne Hill, Ellen Schweitzer, Matthew McClure

NUTRITION NOTES: Margaret Nofziger, Nutritionist for the Farm

PRODUCTION MANAGER: Jane Ayers

ART: James Hartman, Gregory Lowry, Mark Schlichting, Peter Hoyt, Richard Decker, Paul Heavens, Jane Severson, Kathy Koberstein, Nancy Leffer

COMPOSING: Marcia Slaten, Jane Ayers

LAYOUT: Tortesa Livick, Katherine Watrous, James Egan, Susan Seward, Lee Irene Meltzer, Jody Scheflin

DARKROOM AND PHOTOGRAPHY: Brian Hansen, Vance Glavis, Mark Schlichting, Valerie Epstein, Clifford Chappell, Jenny Banks, Lisa Brinkman, Paul Barnett, David Frohman

LITHOGRAPHY: Jeffrey Clark, Valerie Dyess, Thomas Malamed-Durocher, Bill Brothers, Jody Scheflin, Nancy Holzapfel, Daniel Luna

PRINTING AND PRODUCTION: Robert Seidenspinner, John Seward, Michael Tassone, Albert Livick, Steve McGee, Martin Reed, Stephen Swain, Keith Martin

Recipes contributed by:

Jane Ayers, Janie Baldwin, Elizabeth Barger, Albert Bates, Cynthia Bates, Uncle Bill, Letitia Coate, Cynthia Cohen, Judith Dodge, Barbara Elliott, Marsha Ellis, Mary Felber, Anita Figallo, Judith Fox, Edine Frohman, Ina May Gaskin, Stephen Gaskin, Louise Hagler, Michael Halpin, Maureen Hedrick, Elizabeth Houston, Carol Hoyt, Jane Hunnicutt, Janice Hunter, Karen Jordan, Roberta Kachinsky, Richard Lanham, Denise Lichtman, Marion Lyon, Cornelia Mandelstein, Ron Maxen, Marna McKinney, Chris Miller, Janet Mundo, Margaret Nofziger, Samuel Piburn, John Pielaszczyk, Laurie Praskin, Carol Pratt, Ellen Schweitzer, Melanie Splendora, Barbara Swain, Patrick Thomas, Ruth Thomas, Serge Torrez

Art Contributors:

Jeanne Purviance, Michele Murchison, Bonnie Kaufman, Edith Lucas, Tobi Lavender Charles Phillips

Special thanks to:

Dr. Keith Steinkraus, Dr. C. W. Hesseltine, Dr. Hwa Wang, Earl Swain

First Edition — © 1975 The Book Publishing Company
Revised Edition — © 1978 The Book Publishing Company
All rights reserved.
ISBN 0-913990-18-3

Other books available from The Book Publishing Company:
Volume One: Sunday Morning Services on The Farm, by Stephen Gaskin
. . . this season's people, by Stephen Gaskin
Spiritual Midwifery (Revised Edition), by Ina May Gaskin
A Cooperative Method of Natural Birth Control (Second Edition, Revised), by Margaret Nofziger
The Big Dummy's Guide to C.B. Radio, by Albert Houston and the Radio Crew
SHUTDOWN: Nuclear Power On Trial, by Dr. John Gofman & Dr. Ernest Sternglass

The Book Publishing Company
156 Drakes Lane, Summertown, Tennessee 38483

The Farm
Vegetarian Cookbook

Revised Edition

Edited
by
Louise
Hagler

The Farm is a religious vegetarian community of about 1,100 folks living on 1750 acres in southern middle Tennessee, and this is our family cookbook. We are trying to live a self-sufficient lifestyle that is comfortable, graceful and fun, and at the same time one that would be within the reach of everyone on the planet. We have been on the land for seven years as a community after having migrated to Tennessee from San Francisco. The original group came together through open meetings held by Stephen, who is the Farm's founder and minister.

We are vegetarians because one-third of the world is starving and at least half goes to bed hungry every night. If everyone was vegetarian, there would be enough food to go around, and no one would be hungry.

Some of us have been vegetarians together for as long as 13 years, and over these years we have been develop-ing and refining our diet. We have been researching, study-ing, and testing to make sure that what we eat supplies our bodies with everything they need; we have been developing recipes that are tasty, nice looking, and somewhat familiar in taste and texture. We have learned how to make most of our old favorite recipes with vegetarian in-gredients, including burgers, lasagne, eggless cakes, pizza, and barbequed gluten ribs. (Incidentally, there is no cholesterol in the vegetable kingdom.) Ethnic foods seem to adapt easily to vegetarian cooking, and add a spicy variety to our meals. It is traditional in many cultures to combine beans and grains in a meal: beans and corn in Central and South America, lentils and rice in the Middle East. Combining these foods enhances the protein quality of both.

We are completely vegetarian. We eat no meat, fish, poultry, eggs, or any kind of animal dairy products. Our diet is based on the soybean, which we eat in many  different forms, along with other legumes, grains, fruits and vegetables. We grow our own food and recommend it whenever possible. Growing your own is very satisfying, healthful, and inexpensive.

Although most beans need to be combined with a grain for maximum protein, soybeans can stand alone. The protein of soybeans is as growth-promoting as animal products.

The soybean is a noble and versatile bean. We eat soybeans in burritos or burgers or straight from the bowl. In our soy dairy we produce soymilk, which we drink and make into ice cream, yogurt, frogurt, tofu, and other soy cheeses. We also make soybeans into tempeh, a very tasty cultured bean cake.

All in all, we find it to be a satisfying and nutritious diet, and we hope you have a good time cooking and eating this good food.

TABLE OF CONTENTS

Buying Your Beans

You can buy your soybeans at a farmer's supply store. Prices are cheaper when you buy in larger quantities rather than buying small bags at higher prices. A one-bushel (60 lbs.) sack of seed grade beans is enough to last an average family of four well over a month. They will be uniform, clean, high quality beans with good germination in case you want to sprout them. It will be much cheaper to buy beans this way than in other stores. *If you buy your soybeans from a feed or seed store, **be sure** that they have not been treated with mercury or any other poisonous chemical.* Mercury poisoning can be fatal or cause permanent central nervous system damage.

Store your sack of beans tightly closed in a cool, dry place. Always hand sort beans before cooking, because even the best seed cleaner occasionally passes a soybean-sized rock.

Our recipes are based on the commercial oilseed type of soybean, which is the major type grown in this country. There are also vegetable type soybeans which are larger, cook quicker, and are generally more expensive. Different varieties of soybeans have slightly different flavors.

Cooking Your Beans

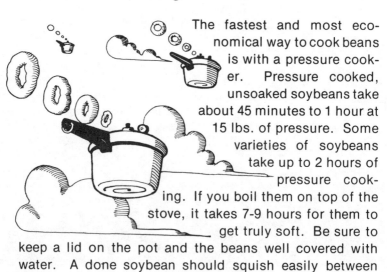

The fastest and most eco-nomical way to cook beans is with a pressure cook-er. Pressure cooked, unsoaked soybeans take about 45 minutes to 1 hour at 15 lbs. of pressure. Some varieties of soybeans take up to 2 hours of pressure cook-ing. If you boil them on top of the stove, it takes 7-9 hours for them to get truly soft. Be sure to keep a lid on the pot and the beans well covered with water. A done soybean should squish easily between your tongue and the roof of your mouth. Crunchy beans don't make it and they're not digestible. When whole soybeans are fully cooked, they are soft, juicy, and delicious. If you've never tasted, soft, fully cooked soybeans, you've never *really* tasted soybeans.

A basic recipe to follow when cooking dried beans in a pressure cooker is **2 cups dried beans** to **6 cups water**, plus **1-2 Tbsp. oil** or **margarine** and **1 tsp. salt.** The oil will form a layer on top and help keep loose bean skins from clogging up the steam vent pipe. If you are cooking soaked beans, skim off the loose skins before cooking. If the vent pipe does become clogged with loose skins, turn the cooker off, bring the pressure all the way down, take off the lid, clean out the vent pipe, and skim off any floating bean skins. Then add a little more oil or margarine to the pot and try again. *Be sure to follow the instructions in your pressure cooker manual.* If you want a gravy surrounding the beans, cook them without a lid for 15-30 minutes after pressure cooking. Make sure the beans are always covered with water.

If you tend to get gas from eating beans, try soaking them overnight, then rinse them well before cooking. During warm weather, beans should be set in the refrigerator to soak so they won't sour or start to ferment while soaking.

Split peas should not be pressure-cooked because they froth up too much and will plug the vent hole.

Refer to the chart below for other bean pressure cooking times. Let the pressure drop on its own.

Legume	Unsoaked and Pressure Cooked	Soaked and Pressure Cooked
Soybeans	45 min.-1 hr.	30-40 min.
Pinto beans	1 hr.-1 hr. 15 min.	25-30 min.
Kidney beans	1 hr.-1 hr. 15 min.	25-30 min.
Black beans	45-50 min.	35 min.
Great Northern beans	30 min.	10-12 min.
Navy beans	25 min.	10-12 min.
Garbanzo beans (chick peas)	1 hr.-1 hr. 15 min.	30 min.
Black-eyed peas	30 min.	20 min.
Lentils	30 min.	20 min.

SOYBEANS AND TORTILLAS
(Soybean Burritos)

Cooked soybeans are excellent with tortillas. They are one of our main staples— we eat them this way often and never tire of them.

Cook **soybeans** as directed on page 12.

Tortillas:

Mix together **6 cups flour, 1 tsp. salt,** and **1 tsp. baking powder** (opt.). Make a well and pour in ¼ **cup oil** or **melted margarine** (opt.) and mix again with a spoon. Add ½ **cup warm water** and mix again. Next add about ¾ **cup more warm water** or enough to knead it into bread dough consistency.

Let it rest for about 5 minutes. Form into balls about 1½" in diameter and dip each ball into flour before rolling it out very thin on an unfloured board. Cook on a hot, dry griddle until bubbly and brown-flecked on each side. This won't take long—only a few seconds on a really hot griddle. They are best served right away but can be stacked under a damp cloth and reheated later.

To fix your beans and tortillas, spread **margarine** across the whole tortilla while it's hot. Drain about ⅓ cup beans and arrange in a line across one edge of the tortilla. Spread about **1 Tbsp. hot sauce** along the beans, sprinkle about **2 tsp. nutritional yeast flakes** ☆ over them, and **salt** to taste. Then roll it all up in the tortilla and enjoy it!

Variation: Chopped tomatoes, onions, and shredded lettuce are also good on soybean burritos.

> **Nutrition Notes:** The protein of soybeans is 100% complete according to the amino acid ratios suggested in *Recommended Dietary Allowances*, 1974, National Academy of Sciences.

☆ See page 58.   *Soybean Tortillas*

SOYBURGERS

Makes 16 burgers

Pressure cook **2 cups soybeans.** Drain **5 cups cooked soybeans** through a colander or strainer. Mash the beans with a potato masher and add while mashing:

2 tsp. salt
1 cup uncooked oats or
   1 cup whole wheat flour
½ tsp. pepper
1 Tbsp. garlic powder
2 tsp. oregano
1 tsp. basil
1 onion, finely chopped
1 green pepper, finely chopped (opt.)

Mix well. The batter should be quite stiff. To make patties, roll mix into a small ball, larger than a golf ball but smaller than a tennis ball. Then flatten the ball to ½" thick. Fry in a generous amount of **oil** so they'll be crisp. (Thin patties make better burgers because they stay crisp—thick patties don't get done so well in the middle.)

Serve on *Soft Sandwich Buns* (p.171).

For "Cheeseburgers":

Put a big glob of thick *Melty Nutritional Yeast "Cheese"* (p.59) on your already fried burger and broil for a few minutes.

Soy Fritters with Tofu Tartar Sauce

SOY FRITTERS
Makes 3-3½ dozen

Cook **2 cups dried soybeans,** drain and save the juice. Measure **3 cups cooked beans** and mash.

Combine with the mashed beans:

1½ cups soybean juice
1 cup whole soybeans
2 cups flour
1½ Tbsp. baking powder
1 Tbsp. salt
1½ tsp. garlic powder
2 medium onions, chopped

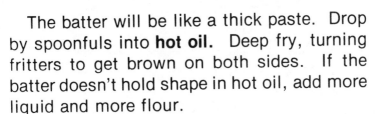

The batter will be like a thick paste. Drop by spoonfuls into **hot oil.** Deep fry, turning fritters to get brown on both sides. If the batter doesn't hold shape in hot oil, add more liquid and more flour.

Serve hot with *Tofu Tartar Sauce* (p.134), *Yogurt Sour Cream* (p.112), or *Tofu Sour Cream* (p.136).

SOYBEAN STROGANOFF

Cook a pot of **soybeans** and a pot of **rice.** For a sauce, to each cup of *Soy Salad Dressing* (p.141), blend in:

¾ tsp. garlic powder
1 Tbsp. soy sauce
3 Tbsp. vinegar

Dish up a serving of soybeans over a serving of rice (more than half beans to rice) and enough sauce to wet the two well on top.

> **Nutrition Notes:** ¾ cup cooked soybeans and ¾ cup cooked brown rice give 21.1 gm. of complete protein.

BARBEQUE SOYBEANS

¼ **cup oil**
3 **medium onions**
3 **cloves garlic,** crushed,
  or **1 tsp. garlic powder**
1 **cup tomato paste**
3 **cups water**
1 **cup sugar**
1 **tsp. molasses**
2 **Tbsp. soy sauce**
½ **tsp. allspice**
2 **Tbsp. salt**
1-2 **crushed red peppers** (about 1-1½ tsp.)
¼ **cup vinegar** or ½ **cup lemon juice**
4 **cups soybeans,** pressure cooked
  and drained

Saute onion and garlic over low flame in oil. Add tomato paste and water and stir well.

Then add, in order, the sugar, molasses, soy sauce, allspice, salt, crushed red peppers, vinegar, and garlic powder (if you don't use whole cloves). Bring to a boil and reduce flame to simmer.

Cook for 15 minutes. Add drained soybeans and stir together. Cook for another 15-20 minutes. It's important to let the soybeans and sauce cook together so that the sauce flavor goes into the beans.

BLACK-EYED PEAS

2 cups black-eyed peas
1 Tbsp. salt
sufficient water for cooking, about 8 cups
Boil 1½ hours, or until beans are soft, but not broken down into gravy.

JANIE'S HOME COOKED CORN BREAD

2 cups cornmeal
2 cups flour (white makes lighter bread)
5 tsp. baking powder
1½ tsp. salt
2 Tbsp. sugar
2¾ cups water or **soymilk**
⅓ cup oil (this is to allow for greasing
    skillet and ¼ cup or so in mix)

Preheat oven to 425°. Try to always have your oven hot. Stick a cast iron skillet in to heat up. It's good if you've fried something in it so it don't take so much oil and the sides are well greased. Used oil is okay to use in this.
Sift the dry stuff (you don't have to but it mixes it up good) and then add the milk or water. Sour milk is excellent, or yogurt (it makes it a little heavier). Stir it up. Put the oil in the hot skillet if it wasn't there already

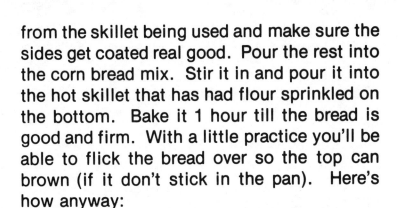

from the skillet being used and make sure the sides get coated real good. Pour the rest into the corn bread mix. Stir it in and pour it into the hot skillet that has had flour sprinkled on the bottom. Bake it 1 hour till the bread is good and firm. With a little practice you'll be able to flick the bread over so the top can brown (if it don't stick in the pan). Here's how anyway:

1. Hold skillet by handle in left hand (make sure you have a good potholder between the handle and your hand).

2. Turn skillet upside down, and if bread don't come out right away, shake it a little. Catch the bread with your right hand and immediately put it back into the skillet, top down, and back to the oven for another 5 minutes or so. When top is brown, remove from oven and put on a plate to be sliced and margarined. Hot margarined corn bread is good with anything, and especially with vegetables and potatoes. If you don't slice and margarine it right away, stick a knife under it so it don't sweat and get soggy.

P.S. You can always brown it in the broiler.

BEATNIK BAKED BEANS

Soak **2 cups pea beans** overnight and cook till tender. Add:

⅓ cup sorghum
1 onion, chopped
1 cup tomatoes, fresh or stewed
1 Tbsp. salt
1 tsp. dry mustard
1/8 tsp. garlic salt
4 Tbsp. oil

Mix well. Bake in a covered dish for 3 hours in a slow oven. Uncover for last hour.

WHITE BEANS
(Pea Beans or Navy Beans)

2 cups white beans
1 onion, chopped
2 tsp. garlic powder
2 tsp. salt
1/8 bay leaf
½ tsp. basil

Pressure cook the beans for 45 minutes. Saute the chopped onion in a little **oil** until transparent and soft and add to the beans, along with the spices. Simmer about 15 minutes and serve.

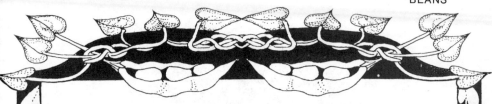

CHILI BEANS AND TORTILLAS
(Burritos)

Pressure cook **2 cups of pinto** or **kidney beans** for about 1 hour. Bring the pressure down and have ready **2** or **3 chopped onions** and **2 cloves pressed garlic** sauteed together. Add these plus **2 tsp. salt**, **2 Tbsp. chili powder** and **2 Tbsp. cumin**. Boil these together for 10-15 minutes.

Fix these tortillas the same as *Soybean Burritos* (p.15). You can add chopped raw onions and pour a strip of *Melty Nutritional Yeast "Cheese"* (p.59) alongside the beans.

> **Nutrition Notes:** 1¼ cups cooked pinto beans + 3 tortillas provide 29.4 gm. of protein. 88% of this protein is complete, giving 25.5 gm. of complete protein.

REFRIED BEANS

Cook **2 cups kidney, pinto,** or **black beans** until soft, and mash with a potato masher. In a large frying pan, saute a **large chopped onion** and **2 cloves pressed garlic** in ½ **cup oil** until transparent; then add mashed beans, mixing well over heat. Add **salt** to taste and continue cooking until thickened and hot. Serve rolled in tortillas with hot sauce and *Melty Nutritional Yeast "Cheese"* (p.59).

BLACK BEAN DIP

Pressure cook for 1 hour:
   2 cups black beans in
   8 cups water
   1 tsp. salt
   While beans are cooking, saute in small skillet:
   2 cups chopped onion in
   ⅓ cup oil
   When onions are soft and slightly browned, turn flame to low and add:
   2 tsp. garlic powder
   1 tsp. cumin
Stir a few minutes and remove from heat.
   When beans are done, drain them, saving liquid. Mash beans well and add:
   sauteed onion mixture
   ¾ cup bean juice
   ½ tsp. hot sauce
   2 tsp. vinegar
   1½ tsp. salt
   Mash well. Serve with chips or on tortillas.

JALA-PINTO DIP

Pressure cook for 1 hour or until soft:
2 cups pinto beans in
8 cups water

Drain beans, reserving ½ cup juice. Saute for 5 minutes:
½ cup chopped onion in
¼ cup oil

Turn flame to very low and add:
1½ tsp. garlic powder
2 tsp. chili powder
½ tsp. ground cumin
¼ tsp. powdered oregano

Cook a few minutes, stirring constantly. Add **¼ cup tomato sauce** and fry a few more minutes. Mash beans. Add tomato sauce mixture and mash some more. Add:
1 tsp. salt
½ cup bean juice
2 tsp. grated raw onion
2 tsp. pickled jalapeno peppers, chopped
1 tsp. pickled jalapeno pepper juice
Whip with whisk. Serve with cornchips.

LENTILS AND RICE

2⅓ cups lentils
6 cups water
1½ tsp. salt
pepper to taste

Cook lentils 35 minutes or until almost done. Add:

1½ cups brown rice
3½ cups water

Cook covered about 45 minutes or until rice is done. In a frying pan, saute **3 medium onions** and **3 garlic cloves** in **⅓ cup oil.** When onions are well cooked and a little browned, add them to the lentils and rice mixture. Stir all together and cook about 5 minutes longer, until flavors are well blended.

RICE AND DAHL

Cook **2 cups yellow split peas** in **6 cups of water** with **2 tsp. salt,** until thick and creamy.

In a small frying pan, saute **2 sliced onions** in ¼ **cup oil** until clear. Turn down the heat and add **3-4 tsp. curry powder.** Add some **more oil** so this mixture isn't dry. Cook the curry powder for a couple of minutes with the onions (don't scorch it). Add the onions and curry to the split peas. Add **vinegar** and more **salt** to taste.

Serve over **rice** with *Soy Yogurt* (see p.108).

KIDNEY BEANS
with SOFRITO AMERICANO

Pressure cook **2 cups kidney beans** in **8 cups water** for an hour. Drain and save **1 cup bean juice.**

Saute until golden:
1 medium onion, chopped
1 green pepper, chopped
in **3 Tbsp. oil**

Turn flame to medium low and add:
1 tsp. powdered oregano
1 tsp. ground cumin
1 tsp. garlic powder
1 tsp. chili powder
1 tsp. fresh cilantro, chopped

Saute spices, stirring constantly, for about 3 minutes, but don't burn! Turn flame to medium heat and add:
1 tsp. salt
1 cup tomato sauce
1 cup bean juice
1 tsp. vinegar
1 tsp. sugar
½ bay leaf

Simmer sauce for 5 minutes. Add sauce to beans in pot. Simmer 10-15 minutes until sauce thickens and flavors blend; stir often. Remove bay leaf. Serve over rice.

Textured vegetable protein is made from defatted soy flour. The soy flour has the oil extracted from it and what remains is mostly protein and carbohydrate. The defatted soy flour is cooked under pressure and extruded through holes, then cut into chunks. This dry precooked food can then be hydrated and cooked into many dishes.

The kind of TVP we usually cook with is granular when dry and hydrates into a shape and texture similar to hamburger. It can be used in any recipe wherever hamburger is called for. Some TVP comes in larger chunks, nice for stews, pot pies, etc.

Helpful Hints for Cooking
Textured Vegetable Protein

It's really important to add the right amount of water to TVP.

**1 cup dry TVP + 7/8 cup *boiling* water =
2 cups hydrated TVP**

After adding the water, stir until all water is absorbed. Soak for 10 minutes.

When browning, stir often to avoid sticking and burning. When forming the mixture into various shapes, be sure to keep your hands wet. This will keep the mixture from sticking.

TVP TORTILLA AND TACO FILLING

Soak **1½ cups TVP** in **1⅓ cups boiling water** for 10 minutes (turn fire off, do not boil the TVP). Saute **1 medium onion**, chopped, with soaked TVP in **5 Tbsp. vegetable oil**. Season with **salt** and **pepper, chili powder, garlic** and **soy sauce**. This can be added to tortillas as is or added to the following tomato sauce for a juicier taco filling:

Taco Filling Sauce

Simmer together:
  2 cups tomato sauce
  ½ tsp. salt
  2 tsp. chili powder
  ½ tsp. pepper
  4 cloves or 2 tsp. garlic powder
  1 Tbsp. sugar
Serve the mixture on a white flour tortilla or a taco shell with shredded lettuce, diced onions, and tomatoes.

CHILI DOGS

Makes about 16

Make a half recipe of *Soft Sandwich Bun* dough (p.171) and let rise. Soak **2 cups TVP** in **1¾ cups boiling water** and **½ tsp. salt** for 10 minutes. Set aside. Chop **1 large onion** and saute in **4 Tbsp. oil.** Add the TVP and saute a few minutes, stirring constantly to prevent burning. Add:

1 cup tomato sauce	**1 cup water**
¾ cup tomato paste	**½ tsp. salt**
1½ tsp. chili powder	**1 tsp. sugar**
½ tsp. garlic powder	**½ tsp. vinegar**
¼ tsp. powdered oregano	**½ tsp. cumin**

Cook this for about 10 minutes over low heat. Divide dough into two parts. Roll one out into a large rectangle 10 x 20 x 1/8". Spread half of the TVP mixture on top.

Cut the dough in half lengthwise. Roll up from both long sides toward the middle so you have 2 long thin rolls. Slice into 3" pieces. Lift with a spatula onto an oiled cookie sheet. Repeat with other half of dough and TVP. Let rise for 10 minutes. Bake at 350° for 20 minutes. Remove and brush with **margarine.** Kids like these—especially dipped in mustard and ketchup.

SPAGHETTI SAUCE WITH TVP

¼ cup olive oil, margarine, or
   vegetable oil
1 onion
1-2 green peppers
6 cups tomato sauce
3½ tsp. oregano
1½ tsp. sweet basil
½ tsp. allspice
3½ tsp. chili powder (opt.)
½ tsp. hot chili (opt.)
1 bay leaf
¼ heaping tsp. black pepper
3¾ tsp. salt
1¼ tsp. cumin (opt.)
1½ tsp. garlic powder
1¼ cups TVP

Saute onions and peppers until soft, and then add the tomato sauce and all the spices, except garlic powder, and bring to a boil. Simmer about 20 minutes. Add TVP and garlic powder and let sit for 10 minutes while TVP softens. When TVP is soft, serve on spaghetti noodles with *Spaghetti Balls* (p.35) or cubes of *Deep Fried Tofu* (p.124).

SPAGHETTI BALLS (or Burgers)
Makes 36 spaghetti balls

Soak **2 cups dry TVP** in **1¾ cups boiling water** for 10 minutes. Then add:

1 small onion (diced), sauteed in
2 Tbsp. oil

½ tsp. chili powder	**2-3 tsp. salt**
½ tsp. garlic powder	**½ tsp. oregano**
pinch of black pepper	**1 Tbsp. soy sauce**

Add **½ cup white flour** and stir until mixed well. Mold this mixture into balls 1" in diameter. Press firmly. Fry in **oil** until crispy. Serve with *Spaghetti Sauce* (p.34) on noodles.

SLOPPY JOES

Saute **1 large onion**, diced, and **2 medium green peppers**, diced, in **3 Tbsp. oil.**

Add:

1½ cups boiling water	**2-3 tsp. salt**
2½ cups tomato sauce	**1 Tbsp. soy sauce**
	1 Tbsp. mustard
1-2 Tbsp. chili powder	**2 Tbsp. sugar**
good pinch pepper	**1½ cups dry TVP**

Simmer together for 20 minutes and serve hot over *Soft Sandwich Buns* (p.171).

TVP GRAVY (with Mashed Potatoes)

Have ready: **1 cup TVP** soaked in **7/8 cup boiling water**; **3 cups very warm soymilk.**

Saute **1 medium onion**, chopped, in **¼ cup oil** until soft. Remove from heat and mix in **½ cup flour**, then whisk in **⅓ cup cold water** until smooth. Next whisk in soymilk and return to medium heat, stirring occasionally till sauce thickens. Cook 10 minutes more over low heat. Then whisk in the TVP with: **¼ cup nutritional yeast flakes** ☆, **1½ tsp. salt, ½ tsp. pepper, 1 tsp. celery seed,** and **2 Tbsp. margarine.** Serve hot over mashed potatoes.

☆ See page 58.

CHILI WITH BEANS
(American Style)

Pressure cook **1¼ cups dry pinto beans.**
Soak **1 cup dry TVP** in **7/8 cup boiling water.** Stir well.

Add **½ tsp. garlic, ½ tsp. chili powder, 1½ tsp. salt.** Stir well, then let soak for 10 minutes.

Saute **1 small onion,** diced, and **1 clove garlic** in **2 Tbsp. oil.** Add the TVP mixture and brown for 2-5 minutes.

Bring to a boil:
  1 cup water
  2 tsp. salt
  pinch black pepper
  1½ cups tomato sauce
  1 cup bean juice
  1-2 Tbsp. chili powder
  1 tsp. sugar
  1 tsp. cumin

Add **2½ cups cooked pinto beans** and the TVP mixture to the tomato base and cook for 5 minutes.

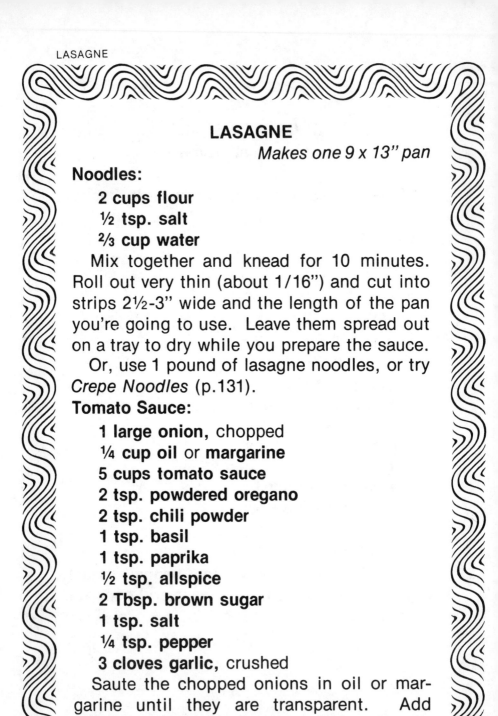

LASAGNE
Makes one 9 x 13" pan

Noodles:

>   **2 cups flour**
>   **½ tsp. salt**
>   **⅔ cup water**

Mix together and knead for 10 minutes. Roll out very thin (about 1/16") and cut into strips 2½-3" wide and the length of the pan you're going to use. Leave them spread out on a tray to dry while you prepare the sauce.

Or, use 1 pound of lasagne noodles, or try *Crepe Noodles* (p.131).

Tomato Sauce:

>   **1 large onion,** chopped
>   **¼ cup oil** or **margarine**
>   **5 cups tomato sauce**
>   **2 tsp. powdered oregano**
>   **2 tsp. chili powder**
>   **1 tsp. basil**
>   **1 tsp. paprika**
>   **½ tsp. allspice**
>   **2 Tbsp. brown sugar**
>   **1 tsp. salt**
>   **¼ tsp. pepper**
>   **3 cloves garlic,** crushed

Saute the chopped onions in oil or margarine until they are transparent. Add remaining ingredients and simmer about 15 minutes, stirring occasionally.

Boil the noodles in **salted water** until tender (about 10 minutes). Drain and rinse in cold water. (If using *Crepe Noodles,* don't boil them—lay them flat in a pan and layer as described below.)

To build lasagne in an oiled baking pan, start with a thin layer of Tomato Sauce, covered with a layer of noodles, next a layer of crumbled **tofu** (p.116). **Salt** this layer, next a layer of Tomato Sauce, then pour a layer of *Melty Nutritional Yeast "Cheese"* (p.59), then repeat, starting with noodles and ending with a generous layer of *Melty "Cheese."*

Bake at 350° for about 35-40 minutes.

EGGPLANT "PARMESAN"

Slice an **eggplant** into rounds ½" thick and coat with **salted flour.** Fry in **hot oil** until browned on both sides and soft. Spread with *Tomato Sauce* (p.38) and top with a thin layer of *Melty Nutritional Yeast "Cheese"* (p.59). Broil until melty cheese bubbles and browns. Serve hot.

Pizza Sauce:

1 small onion
3 Tbsp. oil
4 oz. tomato
  paste
1 cup water
¾ tsp. garlic
  powder
1 tsp. oregano
1½ tsp. chili
  powder
2 pinches all-
  spice
1 pinch black
  pepper
½ tsp. basil
small pinch
  cayenne
  (optional)
½ tsp. salt
5 tsp. sugar

Fry the onion in oil until transparent. Add the rest of the ingredients and simmer for about 15 minutes. Makes one cookie sheet size pizza.

Pizza Dough:
- ⅔ **cup warm water**
- ½ **Tbsp. baking yeast**
- ½ **tsp. salt**
- 2 **tsp. sugar**
- 2 **Tbsp. oil**
- 2⅓ **cup flour**

Sprinkle yeast, salt, sugar and oil over the warm water, and let rest until yeast foams. Mix in flour, and knead for about 10 minutes, then let rise until double. Roll the dough out to fit a cookie sheet or a large pizza pan. It will be a pretty thin skin. Spread this with the sauce and any of the following: ½" slices of **salted tofu, crumbled tofu,** cooked and spiced **TVP, tempeh strips, soysage patties** or pieces of **gluten roast.** Garnish with **onion rings, bell pepper slices, hot pepper slices, fennel seeds, oregano, olives, mushrooms** or **parsley.** Pour strips of *Melty Nutritional Yeast "Cheese"* (p.59) over the top and bake at 500° for 15-20 minutes. Place pizza in the broiler for a few minutes to slightly brown the "cheese" sauce.

CHILI RELLENOS

To prepare **fresh green chilies,** roast about 12 under the broiler or on the griddle, turning them until the skin puffs up all around. Put them immediately in a paper bag, close it up and let them sweat for 20 minutes. Then pull them out one at a time and pull off the skins and remove the seeds and veins. (Commercially prepared chilies may be used instead.) Fill each pepper either with crumbled, sauteed **tofu** (p.116) or with thick *Melty Nutritional Yeast "Cheese"* (p.59). Dip each stuffed pepper in a batter of:

    1½ cups flour
    1 cup water
    2 tsp. salt
    ¼ tsp. pepper

Deep fry in **hot oil** until golden brown. Drain on absorbent paper and serve.

(Mexican Corn)

Yields 28 cups

This is the basis of almost all Mexican cooking. If you use a lot, you'll need this recipe:

10 cups hard field corn
25-30 cups water
3 scant Tbsp. autoclaved finish lime

Mix in a large pot, bring to a boil, then simmer, covered, for 2 hours. Leave standing, hot and covered, for 4 or 5 hours or overnight. (Unsoaked corn can be pressure cooked at 15 pounds pressure for 1 hour.) Drain and rinse corn in small batches in a colander under running water, rubbing corn vigorously between palms of hands to remove most of the outer hulls. Finished yellow corn should be bright, shiny and yellow. Corn should be soft, only very slightly chewy.

Small Batch — yields 7 cups:

2½ cups corn
7½ cups water
1½ tsp. lime

Proceed as above, but simmer for 3 hours. If you have a wood stove, try leaving it on the stove overnight with lots of water and a good cover.

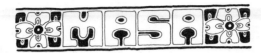

The dough made from grinding the nixta-mal into a paste is called *masa*. The grinding can be done at home by a hand food-grinder on a tight setting. It should come out a smooth paste that can be kneaded. The dough will sour, so it should be cooked in some form right away or refrigerated. Cooked tortillas will keep several days.

TORTILLAS

Knead the **masa** until it is all one lump, firm and moist. If it's dry, sprinkle **water** over the dough as you knead it. If it is too wet, knead in some **flour.** The dough should not stick to your hands. You can also knead in ½ **tsp. salt** to each cup of masa.

There are several different methods that can be used to shape the tortillas. Our Central American friends take a small ball of the dough and slap-pat it into tortilla shape with their hands.

Another way is to put a small ball of dough between two layers of plastic sheet (a bread bag or heavy plastic bag is a good weight) and smash it with a flat bottom fry pan on a smooth surface. There are also commercial hand tortilla presses that will work well along with the plastic sheets.

Still another way is to form a ball about 1¼" in diameter and place it between the two layers of plastic sheet. With a rolling pin, roll this flat and round, turning from one side to the other as it curls up. Be careful to roll the tortilla to an even thickness and pull off the plastic.

To Cook the Tortillas:

As you finish pressing each tortilla, lay it on a hot, dry griddle that has been lightly salted. When the edges curl up and they bubble up in the middle, flip them over to cook on the other side (about 1-1½ minutes on each side). They will have toasted brown flecks.

Tortillas are good to eat hot off the griddle plain, spread with margarine, rolled up with beans, crumbled tofu, chopped lettuce, tomatoes, pickles, hot peppers, hot tomato salsa, nutritional yeast flakes ☆, etc., or any combination that turns you on. For tacos, fry the tortillas in oil until crisp and top with any of the fillings above. Also try *TVP Taco Filling* (p.32).

CORN CHIPS

Cook thinly rolled **tortillas** lightly on one side on a hot, dry griddle. Cut these tortillas in quarters and deep fry till crispy. Drain and **salt** while hot.

☆ See page 58.

MICHAEL'S TAMALES
Yields about 20 tamales

Dough:

7 cups nixtamal (small recipe on p.44)
¼-½ lb. margarine
1 Tbsp. salt
¼ cup water

Grind nixtamal into a paste at tight setting of Corona or similar hand grinder. Knead in salt, water and margarine. The dough should be firm but moist. You can use dried "masa de harina" mix, enough to make about 4½ cups of a moist pasty dough, and then add margarine. (Salt the water you use to mix it.)

Filling:

3 Tbsp. margarine
5 cloves garlic, finely minced
1 Tbsp. fresh thyme, chopped
2 Tbsp. fresh parsley, chopped
1-2 jalapeno peppers, minced
1 cup tomato puree
1 Tbsp. salt
1 tsp. ground cumin
½ cup TVP

Saute garlic, thyme and parsley in margarine over very low heat for 5 minutes. Add peppers, tomato puree, salt and cumin. Simmer 5 more minutes. Stir in TVP and turn off heat.

To assemble:

Cut the stem of an ear of corn so that the shucks peel off without splitting.

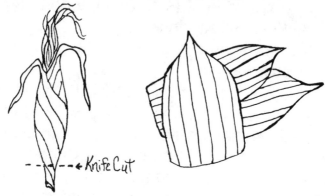

← Knife Cut

Take one wide, long husk or two small ones pasted together with a little tamale dough. Then spread some more dough about 1/8-1/4" thick on the corn husk like this:

1. Place a little filling, which should not be too soupy, but should be juicy, in the middle of the dough. Sprinkle some grated imitation American cheese (optional) over the filling. Fold the right side of the tamale to the center of the dough.

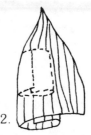

2. Fold the left side over till the left edge of the dough meets the right edge, and press lightly to cause the edges to join. Continue wrapping the left edge of the husk around the tamale.

3. Pinch the ends of the tamale so that the dough closes up the opening at the ends. Fold the top down and the bottom up.

4. Stack the tamales in a basket or on a rack in a pot to keep them out of the water. Stack with flaps down to keep the tamales from unwrapping while cooking. Stack loosely to allow the steam to flow around them. Steam in a covered pot for 1-1½ hours or pressure cook on a rack 40 minutes. When done and slightly cooled, the unwrapped tamale should be tender and nut-like in flavor. It should be firm enough to eat with your fingers.

ENCHILADAS

Prepare **12-14 masa tortillas** (p.45).

Chili Gravy:

- 6 Tbsp. oil
- 1 large onion, chopped fine
- 3 cloves garlic, chopped fine, or
  - 1½ tsp. garlic powder
- 1¼ tsp. salt
- ¾ tsp. cumin
- 6 Tbsp. chili powder
- 6 Tbsp. white flour
- 1½ quarts water

Fry onions in oil until soft. Mix in everything but water, then beat in water with a wire whip, to keep from lumping. Boil 20 minutes.

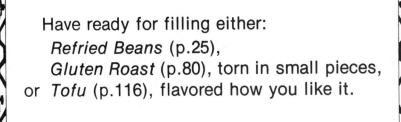

Have ready for filling either:
  Refried Beans (p.25),
  Gluten Roast (p.80), torn in small pieces,
or *Tofu* (p.116), flavored how you like it.

Fixing one tortilla at a time, drop the cooked tortilla in **hot oil** for a couple of seconds on each side, so it comes out flexible, then dunk it in the *Chili Gravy,* and lay it on a plate. Lay a strip of one of the abovementioned fillings across the tortilla, then roll it up. Cover the bottom of a 9 x 13" baking pan with *Chili Gravy* (about 1 cup), line the pan with the rolled tortillas and pour the rest of the gravy over the top. Next pour wide strips of *Melty Nutritional Yeast "Cheese"* (p.59) over the top. Bake at 350° for about 25 minutes.

TAMALE PIE

4 cups dried field corn
12 cups water
4 tsp. autoclaved finish lime
1 Tbsp. salt
Pressure cook for 1 hour. Then rinse the corn in a colander under running water, rubbing the corn vigorously between palms of hands to remove the brown outer hulls. Finished yellow corn should be bright, shiny and yellow. Grind the corn, adding enough warm water to make a stiff but movable paste.

Pressure cook:
  3 cups pinto beans
  water to cover well (about 9 cups)
  1 Tbsp. oil

Cook for 1 hour, until soft, then drain and save the water. Saute in ⅓ **cup oil** until soft:
  2 medium onions
  2-3 green peppers

Then add:

   3 cups canned tomatoes
   3 Tbsp. cumin
   4 Tbsp. chili powder
   3 tsp. oregano
   3 tsp. salt
   ¼ tsp. pepper
   1½ tsp. garlic powder
   2 cups bean juice
   3-6 canned green chilies and **juice**

In a deep casserole dish, put a ½" layer of corn paste, then pour in a 1" layer of beans. Over this, spread a thin layer of hot sauce.

Bake at 350° for about ½ hour, until it has heated through. It should be solid like tamales.

JANE'S "GRINGO POSOLE"

Combine:
3 cups dried corn
9 cups water
1 Tbsp. lime

Pressure cook for 1 hour or boil for 3 hours. Rinse *well,* until water runs clear, and drain. Then place corn in soup pot. Add and simmer 2-3 hours:

3 cups tomato sauce	**2 cups water**
1 tsp. sweet basil	**½ tsp. oregano**
1 tsp. coriander leaf	**1 tsp. cumin**
("Mexican parsley")	**¼ tsp. thyme**
1/8 tsp. cayenne pepper	**1 Tbsp. sugar**

Saute in **2 Tbsp. margarine** or **oil**:
2 jalapeno peppers, cut up
1-2 carrots, cut up (optional)
1-2 stalks celery, cut up (optional)
1 tsp. salt
1 clove garlic, minced fine
2 medium onions, sliced
1 cup chopped collards or **cabbage**

Add sauteed mixture to the soup. Simmer another 40 minutes. This chowder is traditionally served sprinkled with chopped raw onion, radish, and lettuce.

CHILEQUILES
ESTILO DE SAN LUIS POTOSI

Serves 6

These are traditionally quite hot, and are served with **refried pinto beans** for breakfast.

2 dozen corn tortillas
1 medium onion, diced
½ cup oil
3 small cloves garlic, pressed
salt and **pepper** to taste
¾ cup hot sauce
1½ cups fried yuba* (optional)

Tear the tortillas into bite-size pieces, about 1" or 1½" square. Fry the onion at medium-high heat till *slightly* golden in a large skillet, using about half the oil. Add the tortilla pieces and continue frying till all the pieces are golden and crisp. You may need to add more oil. Lightly sprinkle with salt and pepper. Add the garlic and hot sauce, stir once and cover immediately. Steam for 2 or 3 minutes, remove lid. Add remainder of oil and continue to fry, tossing and stirring chilequiles till they are slightly crispy again. Add fried yuba and taste for salt and pepper, adding more if needed. Remove from heat and serve hot.

*Yuba—see page 142.

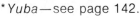

CORN PUFFS

1 cup masa
1 tsp. baking powder
½ tsp. salt
2 Tbsp. nutritional yeast flakes ☆
1 Tbsp. flour

Mix dry ingredients, knead well into masa. Form the dough into little logs ½" in diameter and 2-3" long. Deep fry and drain.

MASA DUMPLINGS

1 cup masa
½ tsp. baking soda
1 tsp. salt
¼ cup white flour
1 tsp. baking powder
2 Tbsp. sugar (for sweet dumplings only)

Mix dry ingredients, sprinkle onto masa and knead until well mixed. Form into balls 1¼-1½" in diameter and drop a few at a time into plenty of rapidly boiling water. Cook at a good simmer uncovered about 15 minutes. Break one open with a fork to see if it's done. It should be like fresh corn bread inside with a wet layer outside. Serve as part of a main meal, or as a hot dessert with fruit sauce or syrup.   ☆ See page 58.

ATOLE

Atole is a hot drink, or cooled down,
a light pudding

Put a **ball of masa** about 4" in diameter in a bowl and gradually knead in enough **water** or **soymilk** to form a smooth lumpless batter. There should be about 3 cups of batter at this point. Add **3 more cups water*** and **1½ tsp. salt** and mix well. Bring this to a boil in a double boiler, stirring carefully. Remove from heat, add **sweetener** to taste, a lump of **margarine**, and **flavoring** such as vanilla, almond, mashed banana, lemon, cinnamon, or cocoa.

*You may need to add more water depending on how wet or dry the masa was to start with. If you are going to drink it, it should be thin enough to drink. If you are making pudding, it should stand up slightly when dropped from a spoon.

☆ *Nutritional Yeast* ☆

We eat nutritional yeast regularly for its good quality protein and B vitamins. The kind we use is *Saccharomyces cerevisiae,* a food yeast grown in a molasses solution. This yeast is easily digestible and contains all the essential amino acids. It has a yellow or gold color from its riboflavin content. This yeast contains:

Protein	40%
Fat	1.2%
Carbohydrate	31.5%

B vitamins:

Percentage of U.S.R.D.A. in 2 Tbsp. yeast flakes (9 gm.) or 1 Tbsp. yeast powder (9 gm.):

Thiamin	386%
Riboflavin	337%
Niacin	175%
Vitamin B12	150%
Vitamin B6	270%
Folic Acid	29%

It tastes cheesy in spreads, sauces, salad dressings, crackers, breading meal, and on vegetables and popcorn. Added to soups, gravies and gluten, it has a good, nutty flavor. You can add it to your baby's food, too. Store in a cool, dark place.

This yeast comes in both flakes and powder form. In a recipe calling for flakes, you can use half as much powder.

☆ **Do not** use brewer's yeast or torula yeast in any of these recipes. Use only *Saccharomyces cerevisiae.* It comes in golden or bright yellow flakes or powder. If you use any other kind, these recipes will not taste the same. ☆

MELTY NUTRITIONAL YEAST "CHEESE"

1 cup nutritional yeast flakes ☆
⅓ cup white flour   **½ tsp. garlic**
1½ tsp. salt   **powder** (opt.)
2 cups water   **2 tsp. wet**
¼-½ cup margarine   **mustard** (opt.)

Mix dry ingredients in a saucepan. Gradually add water, stirring with a whisk, making a smooth paste and then thinning with the remaining water. Place on heat and stir constantly until it thickens and bubbles. Let it bubble for about 30 seconds and remove from heat. Whip in the margarine (and mustard).

The sauce may get thick if it sits for a while. If so, heat it up and whip in a small amount of water.

Variation: For a richer, stretchier sauce that's good on pizza, substitute for the flour **3 Tbsp. cornstarch** and **1 Tbsp. flour**, whip in **1 cup oil** instead of margarine, and add as much as **1 cup more water** at the end, as needed to make a thick, smooth, pourable sauce. Pour it on your pizza and for the last few minutes of baking, put it under the broiler until it forms a stretchy, golden-brown speckled skin.

☆ See page 58.

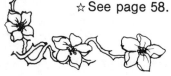

CHEEZY CRACKERS

2 cups flour
2 tsp. baking powder
½ tsp. salt
1 tsp. garlic
1 tsp. chili powder
⅔ cup nutritional yeast flakes ☆
⅔ cup water or soymilk
1 Tbsp. soy sauce
3 Tbsp. oil

Preheat oven to 425°. Mix the dry ingredients. Mix in oil, then water (more if needed) and soysauce to make a stiff dough. (If soy sauce is not used, double the salt.) Knead until the dough is a smooth ball. Roll 1/16" thick, oil top of dough and sprinkle with salt. Cut into shapes. Bake until both sides are golden brown (7-10 minutes) at 425°.

☆ See page 58.

YEAST CREPES

2 cups flour
¾ cup nutritional yeast flakes ☆
½ tsp. baking powder
1 tsp. salt
3-3½ cups water *
2 Tbsp. melted margarine
1 cup mashed tofu (optional)

Whisk ingredients, except tofu, together until smooth. Whisk in mashed tofu. Pour ¼ cup of this batter into a medium hot 9" crepe pan (or cast iron frying pan) that has been coated with margarine. Tilt the pan all around so that the batter forms an even layer over the whole pan. Cook over medium high heat until the edges of the crepe come away from the side of the pan, the top starts to dry out and bubble up. Loosen and flip the crepe over and cook the other side until it is golden flecked. Spread with margarine, fold in thirds and eat.

Or, fill the middle with flavored tofu, TVP, or beans, and hot salsa.

☆ See page 58.

*This varies depending on the type of flour you use. The batter should be thin enough to spread around the pan easily and thick enough that they don't fall apart when flipped.

MACARONI AND "CHEESE" CASSEROLE

Serves 5

Cook **3½ cups elbow macaroni.**

In a saucepan, melt **½ cup margarine** over low heat. Beat in **½ cup flour** with a wire whisk and continue to beat over a medium flame until the mixture (called a *roux*) is smooth and bubbly. Whip in **3½ cups boiling water, 1½ tsp. salt, 2 Tbsp. soy sauce, 1½ tsp. garlic powder,** and a **pinch of turmeric,** beating well to dissolve the **roux.**

The sauce should cook until it thickens and bubbles. Then whip in **¼ cup oil** and **1 cup nutritional yeast flakes** ☆.

Mix part of the sauce with the noodles and put in casserole dish, and pour a generous amount of sauce on top. Sprinkle top with **paprika** and bake for 15 minutes in a 350° preheated oven. Put in broiler for a few minutes until "cheese" sauce gets stretchy and crisp.

☆ See page 58.

BUCKWHEAT GROATS AND GOLDEN GRAVY

Groats:

Lightly toast groats in a little **oil** in frying pan or on a cookie sheet in the oven until browned and aromatic. Add **2 parts boiling water.** Cover and cook over a low heat until the water is absorbed, about 15 minutes. Don't stir while they're cooking.

Golden Gravy:

½ cup nutritional yeast flakes ☆
¼ cup flour
⅓ cup oil
1½ cups water
2-3 Tbsp. soy sauce
¾ tsp. salt
1/8 tsp. pepper

Toast the yeast and flour until you can start to smell it. Add the oil and stir while it bubbles, and turns golden brown. Add water, still stirring with a whisk, until it changes to gravy consistency. Stir in soy sauce, salt and pepper.

☆ See page 58.

KNISHES

Dough:

Combine:

1 cup cooked potatoes, peeled and mashed

¼ cup oil

1 tsp. salt

Add:

3 cups flour, mixed with

1 tsp. baking powder

Mix well. Make a well in the center of the flour mixture and add **½ cup cold water.** Knead into a smooth dough. Let rest on a lightly floured board and cover with a bowl or cloth for ½ hour.

Cut dough into 4 sections. Roll as thin as possible. Cut into rectangles about 2 x 3" for regular knishes or smaller for appetizers. Place filling in center of rectangle and fold the two shorter ends toward the center first. Then fold the two longer ends over each other. Bake on a well-oiled baking sheet, fold side down, till golden, about ½ hour in a 350° oven.

Buckwheat Filling:

Roast **3 cups buckwheat groats** until brown.

Combine with:

9 cups boiling water
4 tsp. salt
1 tsp. pepper

Cook over low heat until groats are soft, about 20 minutes. Meanwhile, saute **2 medium onions** (2-3 cups) in **2 cups oil**. Add sauteed onions and oil to cooked groats. Mix well with a fork.

Potato Filling:

Combine and mix well:

1½ cups mashed potatoes
½ tsp. salt
¼ tsp. pepper
½ cup onions, sauteed in
¼ cup margarine

ELLEN'S GOOD FOR YA NOODLE SOUP

Serves 12

2 medium onions	4 Tbsp. soy sauce
5 Tbsp. oil	5-6 cups spaghetti,
6 quarts water	broken into
1 cup green split peas	small pieces
4 bay leaves	4 Tbsp. nutritional
1½ tsp. celery seed	yeast flakes ☆
2 Tbsp. salt	4-5½ cups more water
⅓ tsp. pepper	

Chop the onions, then saute in oil until medium brown. Set aside. Bring water to a boil and add split peas, bay leaves, and celery seed. With lid on, cook the peas until they dissolve and make a light green broth (one hour or so). Then add salt, pepper, soy sauce and onions (scrape the oil they're in and put in soup, too). You will probably have to add the 4-5½ cups more water during the course

of cooking the peas because they boil down a lot. Keep the soup boiling lightly and add the noodles. Cook until tender. Whisk in nutritional yeast.

ONION SOUP

Serves 6

5 cups onions,	**2 tsp. salt**
sliced in rings	**1/8 tsp. pepper**
5 Tbsp. oil	**3-4 Tbsp. soy sauce**
7½ cups water	**3 Tbsp. nutritional**
2½ tsp. tarragon	**yeast flakes** ☆

Fry onions in oil in a cast iron skillet until they're well browned. Meanwhile, put water on to boil. Add onions, tarragon, salt and pepper to boiling water and turn down to simmer slowly for 5-10 minutes.

Add soy sauce and yeast at the end. You can make a lot of this soup and refrigerate it overnight. Sitting overnight enhances the flavor.

☆ See page 58.

MINESTRONE SOUP

Pressure cook **2 cups kidney beans** for 1 hour or until soft. Then saute:

2 onions, chopped
4 stalks of celery, chopped
4 carrots, cut in rounds
1 small cabbage, shredded
1-2 medium potatoes, chopped (opt.)

in **½ cup oil** until limp. If you are going to add potatoes, add them at this time also. Next add:

4 cups stewed tomatoes
2 tsp. garlic powder
2 tsp. oregano
4 tsp. basil
1 Tbsp. salt
½ tsp. pepper
1 Tbsp. dried parsley
8 cups water

When this comes to a boil, add **1 cup noodles** or **cooked rice.**

Boil for 15 minutes, stirring occasionally to keep from sticking. Add the beans and simmer for a few minutes before serving.

PESTO

4-5 cloves garlic
2 Tbsp. dried basil
¼-½ cup oil

Mince garlic very fine or use garlic press. Add basil, then oil, and mix together, rubbing garlic and basil against side of cup so as to get the juices into the oil.

Add to *Minestrone* or pasta before serving.

ROBERTA'S GOOD SOUP

Saute **1 medium onion** (diced) in **3 Tbsp. oil.** Add the onion to:

5 cups boiling water
1 Tbsp. salt
1/8 tsp. black pepper
¼ tsp. celery seed
¼ cup dry TVP
1 tsp. soy sauce

Simmer for 5 minutes. Add:

½ cup nutritional yeast flakes ☆
1½ Tbsp. margarine
2 cups cooked noodles
    or **1-1½ cups cooked rice**

This is a quick and easy soup to make and kids love it. Serve with sprouts and/or crackers.

☆ See page 58.

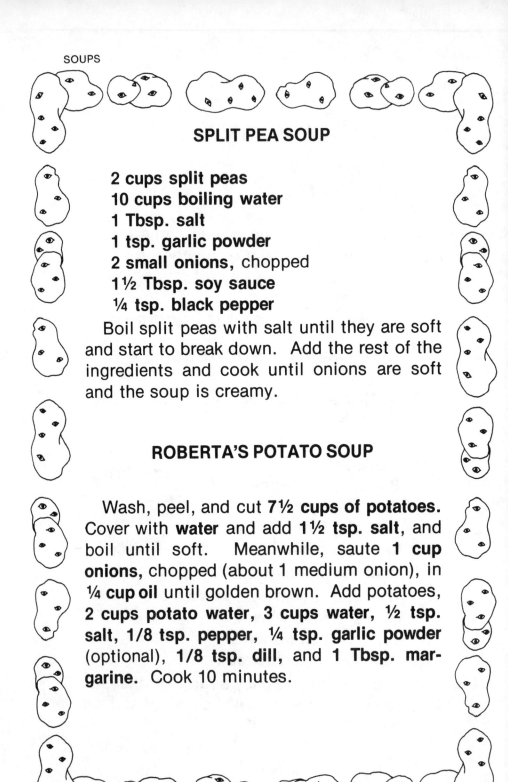

SPLIT PEA SOUP

2 cups split peas
10 cups boiling water
1 Tbsp. salt
1 tsp. garlic powder
2 small onions, chopped
1½ Tbsp. soy sauce
¼ tsp. black pepper

Boil split peas with salt until they are soft and start to break down. Add the rest of the ingredients and cook until onions are soft and the soup is creamy.

ROBERTA'S POTATO SOUP

Wash, peel, and cut **7½ cups of potatoes.** Cover with **water** and add **1½ tsp. salt,** and boil until soft. Meanwhile, saute **1 cup onions,** chopped (about 1 medium onion), in **¼ cup oil** until golden brown. Add potatoes, **2 cups potato water, 3 cups water, ½ tsp. salt, 1/8 tsp. pepper, ¼ tsp. garlic powder** (optional), **1/8 tsp. dill,** and **1 Tbsp. margarine.** Cook 10 minutes.

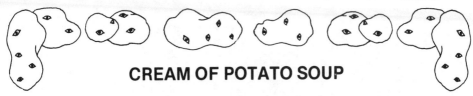

CREAM OF POTATO SOUP

Scrub and cut **10 cups white potatoes.** Boil until soft in **6 cups water** and **2 tsp. salt.**

Meanwhile, saute **1 medium onion** (about 1-1½ cups) in **¼ cup oil.** Add **¼ cup flour** to onions to make a smooth paste. Stir constantly.

Drain potatoes, saving the water. Mash **2 cups potatoes** and add to potatoes in pot, along with:

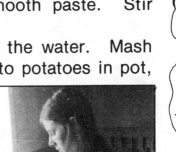

4 cups potato water
2 cups soymilk
onion-flour paste
1½ tsp. salt
¼ tsp. pepper
¼ tsp. dill weed
1 Tbsp. margarine

Cook over low heat 10-15 minutes.

"To feed yourself may even be a sin—it depends on how overweight you are. But to feed someone else is a Holy duty."
—Rabbi Shlomo Carlbach

We feel blessed to have had Uncle Bill live with us the last few years of his life. Born in Poland and brought up in Brooklyn, New York, Uncle Bill spent much of his life as a delicatessen manager and caterer in New York City. He came to the Farm in January 1974 from a nursing home in southern Florida, at age 81.

At first he wasn't used to our way of life and our diet. But in no time he was cooking Jewish dishes, vegetarian style—like making eggplant taste like pickled herring. On most days you would find him tasting, seasoning, mixing, and serving in one of the many kitchens on the Farm. He loved to feed folks, especially the kids. And the parties he would throw—the Farm had never seen the likes of them.

Besides teaching us to eat good and have fun, Uncle Bill taught us about old folks and what a groove they are to have around. We will always remember and love our Uncle Bill.

UNCLE BILL'S
TURNIP APPETIZER

Saute:

2 cups chopped onions in
½ cup oil

until golden brown. Combine:

2 cups finely grated turnips
½ cup oil
1¼ tsp. salt
3/8 tsp. pepper
¼ cup finely grated onion

Add the sauteed onions and mix well.

UNCLE BILL'S
TURNIP CHIPS

Peel and slice into thin chips:

2 cups raw turnips

Mix in:

¼ cup oil
1 tsp. salt
¼ tsp. pepper

Let sit for ½ hour or more
before serving.

UNCLE BILL'S
SAUERKRAUT SOUP
(Sauerkraut Borscht)

Simmer over low heat for 1½-2 hours:

8 cups sauerkraut
8 cups water
1¼ cups sugar
2 cups raisins
1 cup prunes, cut in small pieces
2 thin slices lemon
¼ tsp. salt

Serve hot with **tiny boiled potatoes** in the soup.

ONION ROLLS

2 medium onions,	**⅓ tsp. salt**
chopped fine	**⅓ tsp. dill**
⅓ cup oil	**⅓ tsp. garlic**
1 Tbsp. sugar	**1/8 tsp. pepper**

Saute onions in oil until golden brown. Add spices and fry another minute. Remove from heat. Using *Soft Sandwich Buns* recipe (p.171), make rolls and put on trays. Cover the top of each roll with 1 tsp. of sauteed onion mixture before they rise. Let rolls rise ½ hour and bake at 375° for 20 minutes or until the bottoms are brown and the tops are beginning to brown.

PICKLED "LOX"

Slice **1 medium eggplant** into pieces approximately 2" long, 1" wide, and ¼" thick. Place in a bowl and cover with **salt**. Press with a weight overnight. Drain the water off in the morning. Fry in **⅓ cup oil** until soft but not mushy. Add **2 Tbsp. vinegar, 1 tsp. garlic powder**, and **¼ tsp. pepper**. Fry another minute. Let cool. Serve on bagels with *Soy Cream Cheese* (p.136).

PICKLED "HERRING"

Take the cooled *Pickled "Lox"* and add **1½ cups** *Tofu Sour Cream* (p.136), **1 onion** sliced very fine, and **1 Tbsp. lemon juice**.

GLUTEN

Gluten is the protein part of wheat. It is the stringy stuff that holds bread together. It has a tough elastic texture in its raw form which, with added oil, salt, various spices, and cooking, makes delicious salty, oily, chewy, nutritious things to eat. It has all the things you liked about meat without having to take the life of an animal.

BASIC RAW GLUTEN

8 cups wheat flour*
2 cups water, approximately (enough to make a kneadable dough)

Mix and knead the above together for about 20-30 minutes or until you have a very smooth ball of dough with no cracks in it. Kneading is what develops the gluten. It should bounce back when you punch it. Hard wheat flour and high-gluten flour develop the best.

Put this ball of dough in a bowl large enough to hold it and add enough cold water to cover the ball completely. Let it soak under water for one or two hours. Then begin kneading it under water, kneading out all the starch and being careful to hold the gluten together. Change the water when it gets pretty milky from the starch, and keep changing it until the water stays almost clear. This should make 1½-2 cups of raw gluten which is ready to be spiced, oiled, and cooked. The next few pages give some different ways to prepare it. (See picture of raw gluten on p.78.)

*This can be all whole wheat flour, half and half white and whole wheat flour, half and half gluten flour and whole wheat flour, or all gluten flour, or any combination of wheat flours.

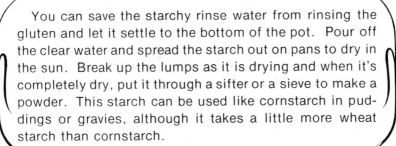

WHEAT STARCH

You can save the starchy rinse water from rinsing the gluten and let it settle to the bottom of the pot. Pour off the clear water and spread the starch out on pans to dry in the sun. Break up the lumps as it is drying and when it's completely dry, put it through a sifter or a sieve to make a powder. This starch can be used like cornstarch in puddings or gravies, although it takes a little more wheat starch than cornstarch.

CHILI GLUTEN

Take **4 cups washed raw gluten** and cut into 3 large chunks. Put in a large pot and cover with **water.** Add:

3 Tbsp. soy sauce
1 cup nutritional yeast flakes ☆
4 Tbsp. margarine   1 tsp. garlic powder
1 Tbsp. salt   2 onions, chopped

Bring to a boil and simmer 45 minutes. Drain the chunks and save the broth. Saute **2 chopped onions** and **1 chopped green pepper** in ¼ **cup oil** in a heavy skillet. When tender, add ⅓ **cup chili powder** and **3 tomatoes,** chopped. Continue frying for about 4-5 minutes.

Chop gluten into bite-size chunks. Add to sauteed mixture, along with ⅔ **cup gluten broth** and **1 tsp. garlic powder.** Cover the skillet and continue cooking for 20 minutes. **Salt** to taste. Remove cover and cook 10 minutes longer.

Serve on tortillas with hot sauce.

☆ See page 58.

GLUTEN ROAST

Add to **2 cups raw gluten:**

½ cup oil   **½ tsp. garlic powder**
¼ cup soy sauce   **1 tsp. onion powder**
1 tsp. salt   **1/8 tsp. black pepper**
½ cup walnuts, peanuts, almonds,
    etc., ground, or **peanut butter**

If necessary to mix all the dry ingredients, grind the gluten in a food grinder. Mix all the ingredients and put in an oiled loaf pan. Cover with equal parts of **oil, soy sauce,** and **water.** Bake at 350° for 1-1½ hours.

Variation: Instead of a loaf pan, use a Dutch oven or roaster, following above recipe. Place **sliced potatoes** and **carrots** around gluten and **sliced onions** on top. Cover with equal portions of **oil, soy sauce,** and **water.** Bake at 350° uncovered for the first half hour, covered for a half hour, and uncovered the last half hour. Baste throughout.

Louise bags a five-pound gluten

OVEN FRIED GLUTEN

1 onion, chopped fine
3 cloves garlic, crushed
½ cup margarine
4 cups washed raw gluten
¼ cup peanut butter or **tahini**
½ tsp. marjoram or **sage**
1½ Tbsp. salt
1-2 tsp. black pepper
1 tsp. paprika
1 cup nutritional yeast flakes ☆

Saute the onions and garlic in the margarine. Add the rest of the ingredients and the hot sauteed onion and garlic to the raw gluten and work them through with your fingers. Take about ⅓ cup piece of gluten and pull and flatten it out till it's about ¼" thick and 3-4" long. Spread about 1 tsp. margarine on this stretched piece and roll it up like a jelly roll, then flatten it out. Next, roll it in a crumb mixture of:

1¾ cups cracker crumbs
1 tsp. garlic powder
½ tsp. salt
¼ tsp. pepper
¼ cup wheat germ

Pour ¼ **cup oil** on a cookie sheet, put the crumbed glutens on it, and bake at 375° for about 1 hour, turning once when golden brown on the bottom. Don't overcook!

☆ See page 58.

JANICE'S
BARBEQUE GLUTEN "RIBS"

4 cups washed
   raw gluten
⅓ cup nutritional
   yeast flakes ☆
½ cup peanut butter
   or sesame tahini
2 Tbsp. paprika

3 Tbsp. salt,
   or to taste
1 large onion,
   chopped and
   sauteed in
⅔ cup margarine

Put gluten in bowl with nutritional yeast, peanut butter, paprika and salt on top. Pour hot sauteed onions and margarine over all. While everything is still warm, mix well with hands until the gluten is in stringy, chunky pieces. The hot margarine breaks the gluten down and helps the seasonings penetrate.

Break the gluten off in good-sized pieces to make 2 x 4" gluten "ribs" by pulling, twisting and flattening them to about ¼-½" thick. Do not roll out or cut, as this makes the gluten like bread instead of being chewy.

Pour ¼-½ **cup oil** onto large cookie sheet. Place "ribs" of gluten on sheet and bake in a 350-400° oven for 1 hour or until very crispy and brown on bottom. Pour about **2 cups** *Barbeque Sauce* (see next page) per sheet over gluten and bake 10 minutes longer.

☆ See page 58.

BARBEQUE SAUCE

1 **medium onion,** chopped
2 **cloves garlic,** minced
⅓ **cup oil** or **margarine**
2½ **cups tomato sauce**
¼ **cup water**
1 **cup sugar** (brown is best)
1 **Tbsp. molasses** (use less
   with brown sugar)
½ **cup mustard**
1 **Tbsp.** + 1 **tsp. salt**
1 **tsp. allspice**
1 **Tbsp. crushed red pepper**
1½ **tsp. dried parsley** or
   1 **spring chopped fresh**
¾ **cup lemon juice**
2 **Tbsp. soy sauce**

Saute chopped onion and minced garlic in oil until onions become clear and golden. A large cast-iron Dutch oven is best for this. Add all but the last two ingredients. Bring to a boil, reduce heat and let simmer for about an hour. Add lemon juice and soy sauce and cook 10-15 minutes longer.

GLUTEN BURRITOS
Fry left-over **roasted gluten** with **chopped onions, chopped tomatoes,** and a little **chili.** Fold into large **flour tortillas** (p.14).

Tempeh

Tempeh is a delicious, high-protein main dish made from soybeans. It has been a staple in Indonesia for centuries. Like cheese, yogurt, and sourdough, tempeh is made by natural culturing; the soybeans are cultured with a mold called *Rhizopus oligosporus*. This form of soybeans contains more riboflavin, niacin, and B6 than unfermented soybeans. The protein in tempeh is partially broken down during fermentation, which makes it highly digestible. Children love it, and its ease of digestion makes it particularly suitable for older folks.

Tempeh is easily made at home with basic kitchen supplies. Lightly cooked, split, hulled soybeans are mixed with tempeh starter and allowed to stand in a warm place overnight. The white cake which forms is a quick-cooking, pleasant-tasting, high-protein food that can be prepared in a variety of ways.

MAKING TEMPEH AT HOME

Yield: 10-12 pieces, 4 x 3 x ½"

Materials You'll Need

Ingredients:
> 2½ **cups dry soybeans,** split and hulled*
> 1 **tsp. tempeh starter**
> 2 **Tbsp. vinegar**

*You can split them in a hand grain mill. As they cook the hulls float up and can be skimmed off. Or, see *Other Methods for Splitting and Hulling Whole Soybeans* on page 86.

Tempeh Containers:

The containers should allow enough air to get in so the tempeh can grow, but not so much that the beans dry out. They should hold and maintain the humidity of the fermenting mass, without drowning the mold.

- **Cake pan:** Stretch a piece of tin foil over the top and punch holes in the foil every inch or so.
- **Plastic bag:** Punch holes on both sides about every inch with a fork. Put in a ½" layer of beans. Place bag on a wire cooling rack so air reaches both sides.

Preparation:

1. Cook the split soybeans for 1½ hours at a bubbling boil, skimming off any bean skins that float to the top. (If some are left, that's okay.)
2. Drain off excess moisture, then knead the beans in a towel until they are surface dry. Put the beans in a dry bowl. Having the beans too wet is the most common cause of a bad batch.
3. When they are cooler than skin temperature, add the vinegar and mix well. Then add the starter and mix very well. (Refrigerate starter package in a closed container.)

4. Firmly pack a ½" deep layer of beans into tempeh container.

Growing the Tempeh:

Set the container in a warm place with a stable 85-95° temperature. 90° is best. Check the temperature occasionally. A sunny window or attic, a high kitchen shelf, or a closet with a drop light are some good incubation places. Don't incubate in a small airtight box, as the mold needs oxygen.

For the first 12 hours, the mold is getting started. At 12-15 hours, water condenses on the cover of the tempeh containers and the white mold begins to show faintly on the beans. The tempeh is now producing heat, so check the temperature and adjust it if necessary.

Almost ready

After 19-23 hours, the tempeh looks like white icing on a cake. In the next 2-3 hours, gray or black spots begin to show, especially around the holes in the container. Gray or black areas are the natural result of sporulation (when the mold forms its "seeds") and are not harmful.

In the last 2-3 hours of the 19-26 hour period, the tempeh gets most of its flavor, so be sure to let it grow long enough.

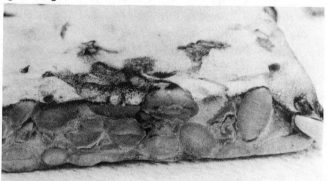

Checking the Tempeh:

Good Tempeh—The beans are solidly bound into a white cake marbled with gray or black. If it's black all over, it has just incubated too long; it's still good to eat unless it smells strongly of ammonia. Fresh tempeh smells good, like bread dough or fresh mushrooms. It may smell faintly of ammonia. A thin slice of tempeh holds together without crumbling. The mold completely fills the spaces between the beans. Good tempeh smells good and feels solid on the bottom.

A slice of good tempeh looks like this

Unfinished tempeh looks like this

Unfinished Tempeh—The mold is usually pure white with no gray areas. The beans are bound together loosely and the mold doesn't fill the spaces between the beans. It crumbles when sliced. Unfinished tempeh doesn't have much flavor when cooked and the beans are a little crunchy. Uneven heat distribution may cause part of the batch to finish late. If this occurs, cut off the finished part and let the rest go longer.

Inedible Tempeh—It smells unpleasant or strongly of ammonia. It may be sticky or slimy all over or in spots. The mold may grow only in patches or not at all. Or it may be well-molded on top, but sticky and unpleasant-smelling underneath or in the middle. (If the beans aren't dry enough, the excess moisture settles to the bottom and the beans spoil.) When pinched, the cake feels mushy or falls apart. Any other color besides white, black or gray tempeh should be thrown away.

Preserving Tempeh:

Small batches of tempeh can be refrigerated for two days. The mold is still alive and producing heat, so be sure not to stack packages of uncooked tempeh on top of each other. Tempeh can be cut into pieces, steamed 5 minutes, and frozen. Thinly sliced tempeh can be sun- or oven-dried and stored without refrigeration, indefinitely.

How to Start Another Batch
of Tempeh from the Previous Batch:

Let some of the tempeh incubate long enough to turn black. Put a piece of it in a small jar of water and shake well. Take out the piece of tempeh—you can cook and eat it. Let the black tempeh spores settle out overnight in the refrigerator and pour off the clear liquid. Then use as directed for dry starter (1 tsp. to 2½ cups dry beans). Check your finished tempeh carefully. After a few batches, use fresh starter. Tempeh starter can be ordered through The Book Publishing Co., Dept. F, 156 Drakes Lane, Summertown, Tennessee 38483. (See also *How to Grow Your Own Tempeh Starter,* p.91.)

Other Methods for Splitting and Hulling Whole Soybeans

Method I: Boil whole dry soybeans 20 minutes. Turn off heat, cover, and let stand for two hours. Then split beans by squeezing them with a kneading motion, a handful at a time, till they're all split. Or, place a thin layer of beans inside a shallow tray; using a closed-mesh potato masher, in a rocking motion, split beans in half. (Some will break up smaller.)

Boil split beans one hour, skimming the hulls. Proceed with step number 2 on page 83.

Method II: Soak beans overnight or by method described above. Chop into large bits with blender or food grinder. Boil 25 minutes (save liquid for use in baking). Proceed with step number 2 on page 83. Place ¼" deep in tempeh container. Pack lightly.

TEMPEH FROM SOY PULP

Squeeze **soy pulp** till dry-moist to touch. Add **vinegar** and **starter** as for soybean tempeh. Place in tempeh containers in ¼" layer, then grow as directed for split soybeans.

BEAN AND GRAIN TEMPEHS

Many beans, grains, and nuts can be used to make tempeh. They should be partially cooked and dehulled or cracked if they have a seedcoat. When cooking, add beans and grains to already **boiling water.** Stir occasionally and skim hulls. Add the **starter** and **vinegar** and package in tempeh container as for soybean tempeh.

Navy beans—Boil 15 minutes, soak 5 minutes in hot water, drain and split with potato masher. Boil 8 minutes, skimming hulls.

Kidney beans—Crack dry beans in half with a mill. Boil 20 minutes.

Great Northern beans—Boil 15 minutes, soak 5 minutes, split with potato masher, boil 6 minutes.

Peanuts—Boil 1½ hours. Use half the recommended vinegar.

Converted rice—Boil 7 minutes, drain, rinse with cold water. Place in tempeh container in ¼" layer. Harvest this tempeh before it grays.

Pearled barley—Boil 15 minutes, drain, rinse with cold water. Package ¼" deep. Harvest when it's still white.

Cracked wheat—Steam 20 minutes, stirring occasionally. Harvest when still white.

You can experiment with nuts, grains, and beans in various combinations. Cook them separately first, then mix together before adding vinegar and starter. Package as for soybean tempeh. These tempehs are delicious pan-fried (see page 88).

RECIPES FOR SOYBEAN TEMPEH

INDONESIAN FRIED TEMPEH

Soak pieces of fresh **tempeh** in **brine** (4 tsp. salt in a quart of water) for 20 minutes. Pan fry in **oil** or **margarine** or deep fry till golden brown. Try it topped with sauce, baked on pizza, or in sandwiches.

Variation: Serve on a margarined roll with *Albert's Tempeh Topping* and sauerkraut.

PAN FRIED TEMPEH

In a skillet, fry squares of **tempeh** in **oil** or **margarine** on one side till golden brown. Add ¼-½ **cup lightly salted water** and cover immediately. When the water steams away, flip the squares. Fry and steam on the other side.

ALBERT'S TEMPEH TOPPING

Serves 6-8

½ **cup tomato paste**	½ **cup sugar**
2 **tsp. hot curry powder**	½ **tsp. salt**

Mix and let stand. Makes 1 cup, enough for one pound of tempeh.

BARBEQUED TEMPEH

Cover the bottom of a **margarined** baking dish with a thin layer of *Barbeque Sauce* (p.81), then cover with pieces of **deep fried tempeh** and then a thick layer of *Barbeque Sauce*. Bake at 350° until it bubbles.

Or, you can baste pieces of deep fried tempeh with the sauce as you grill them over a charcoal grill.

Fried tempeh

SWEET AND SOUR TEMPEH

Cut **tempeh** into strips ½" wide. Deep fry.

Sauce:

- 2 **carrots**, sliced
- 1 **onion**, sliced
- 2 **bell peppers,** chopped
- ⅓ **cup oil**
- ½ **tsp. garlic powder**
- ½ **tsp. ginger**

- ½ **cup water**
- ½ **cup vinegar**
- 2 **Tbsp. soy sauce**
- 6 **Tbsp. sugar**
- 12-**oz. can pine-** apple chunks
- 2 **tsp. cornstarch**
- 2 **tsp. water**

Saute carrots, onions and peppers in oil with garlic and ginger. Mix ½ cup water with vinegar, soysauce, sugar, and juice from canned pineapple. Pour sauce over vegetables and bring to a boil.

Mix cornstarch with 2 tsp. water. When sauce boils, add cornstarch mixture, let thicken, and add pineapple.

Serve tempeh on bed of rice. Pour sauce over it.

CREAMED TEMPEH

Serves 5-6

Place **4 cups tempeh strips** (½" wide and 2" long) in a frying pan. Add **1¼ cups water** and **1¼ tsp. salt,** cover and steam until the water is gone. Remove lid and add **4-5 Tbsp. oil.** Fry at medium heat until golden brown.

To prepare white sauce , melt **5 Tbsp. margarine.** Whisk in **5 Tbsp. white flour** to form a smooth paste, then whisk in **2½ cups soymilk, 1½ tsp. salt,** and a **dash of pepper.** Cook at a low boil for 3 minutes.

Combine tempeh and white sauce, and serve over toast or rice.

TEMPEH CACCIATORE

Serves 6

Steam 12-18 pieces of fresh **tempeh** in a skillet for 5 minutes. Cool. Mix together **½ cup flour, salt** and **pepper.** Dip each piece of tempeh in mixture and fry with **1 cup chopped onions** in **oil** till tempeh is golden brown on both sides. Add the sauce below and simmer 1 hour.

1 quart tomato sauce	**1 tsp. basil**
1 tsp. salt	**1 tsp. oregano**
1 bay leaf	**1/8 tsp. sweet**
2 cloves garlic, minced	**marjoram**
1/8 tsp. thyme	**1 Tbsp. sugar**

Serve with salad and garlic bread.

How to Grow Your Own Tempeh Starter

You can easily grow tempeh starter for your family in your own home kitchen. Basically, what you do is "seed" small medicine bottles containing sterile cooked rice with dried tempeh starter. After the mold grows to maturity, it is used to make tempeh. Using this simple procedure you can grow a fresh supply of tempeh starter indefinitely from one package of dried starter.

When growing cultures, it's important to keep your operation very clean to keep out unwanted micro-organisms. Always work with doors and windows closed as much as possible. Disinfect the work surface, tie your hair back, wear a clean apron, and wash your hands immediately before handling the cultures. Work as close to a lighted burner as safety and practicality permit, because the open flames create an updraft that keeps dust from settling onto your cultures. Assemble all the materials for each section and read the directions carefully before starting.

Starting the Culture from Dried Spore Powder

Materials Needed:

- 1 packet dried tempeh starter
- converted rice
- 1 100-ml. clear glass cough syrup bottle for every 20 lbs. of dry soybeans to be cultured (available from your neighborhood pharmacy)
- pressure cooker and rack
- non-sterile cotton
- paring knife
- alcohol in a small jar
- gas stove burner or alcohol lamp (available from a surgical supply— needs methanol for fuel)
- a long thin-handled spoon
- several small jars with caps

Preparation:

Put 1 Tbsp. white rice and ½ Tbsp. water into each bottle. Lay them on their sides and use the spoon handle to smooth the rice into an even layer on the bottom side of the bottle. Stopper each bottle with a piece of cotton that is firmly packed ½" into the neck and has a large tuft of cotton on the outside, at least 1¼" tall, and wide enough to cover the bottle's lip. Pour 1½" of water into a pressure cooker. Place the bottles on their sides on an elevated rack inside, several inches above the water level.

Cook at 15 pounds pressure for 15 minutes. Bring the cooker down from pressure, remove the bottles, and allow them to stand until cool to the touch.

Seeding the Rice:

Light the gas burner or alcohol lamp. Twist each cotton plug inside the neck of the bottle to loosen it. Open the packet of dried tempeh starter without sticking your fingers down inside the bag. Hold the opened bag in one hand, and with the other hand dip the blade of the paring knife about 3" into the jar of alcohol, then immediately set the blade on fire in your burner flame.

(Caution: Alcohol is extremely flammable. Keep your jar of alcohol as far away from the burner as possible. Cover immediately after use. Always have the cover on hand to put on the jar in case you accidentally set it on fire. Perform this away from flammable materials such as curtains, etc.)

As the knife flames, burning alcohol can drip off the blade, so hold the knife above a nonflammable surface. When the knife is finished flaming, let it cool about 10 seconds. Being careful not to touch the sterile part of the knife to the plastic bag, reach in and pick up a speck of the dried starter on the tip. Put down the bag and pick up the rice bottle. Without touching your skin to the lip of the bottle, grasp the tuft of the cotton plug with the pinkie of your hand holding the knife and pull it out. Here, be careful not to touch the sterile part of the cotton plug against anything unsterile while performing the rest of the operation.

Keep the bottle tilted neck upward and touch the lip of the bottle to the open flame for one full second only. Quickly tap in the dried starter from the knife tip onto the rice. Touch the lip of the bottle to the flame again for one full second. Re-insert the plug, being careful not to touch the lip to your pinkie or to the unsterile part of the cotton. (If you do, reflame the bottle lip and then re-insert the plug.) Turn off the burner. Refrigerate the dried starter packet in a small jar until needed.

Growing the Mold:

Keep the bottles in a warm place (85-90° F.) for 3-5 days. When they turn dark gray to black they're ready to be used for making tempeh. Check each bottle carefully. There should be no other microorganisms visible growing in the rice: no slimy patches, other molds, or any growth other than white, gray, or black.

The rice bottles can be packaged in plastic bags and frozen or refrigerated until needed, or harvested into smaller lots, as described below. The smaller lots can be used immediately to make tempeh, refrigerated for a week, or frozen for long-term storage.

Harvesting the Tempeh Mold:

For every rice bottle you want to harvest, place 5 small empty jars, loosely capped, on a rack in the pressure cooker. Add water to the cooker and cook for 15 minutes at 15 pounds. Bring the cooker down from pressure. Let jars cool.

Light the burner. Flame the handle of a thin-handled spoon. Remove the plug and flame the lip of the molded 100-ml. rice bottle. Use the spoon handle to break up the rice mat. Divide the loose rice evenly among the sterile jars. Cap the jars tightly and put them in plastic bags. Freeze them for long-term storage, or refrigerate.

Each small jar will make 4 pounds of beans, dry weight, into tempeh. When you're ready to make tempeh, add 1 Tbsp. cool water to each rice jar you use and mix well, breaking up any rice clumps. Mix the rice and liquid thoroughly into the cooked, cooled, dried beans in place of the dried starter.

Using this method, you can make hundreds of pounds of tempeh from one packet of dried tempeh starter.

Miso is a traditional fermented food from Japan, made from grain, soybeans and salt. It's similar to soy sauce, but pasty in consistency. In Japan it is most often used as a soup stock for breakfast and other meals. Miso comes in a number of varieties, from light-colored and sweet to dark and robust. It contains healthful microorganisms that aid digestion when eaten with other foods.

Miso is good in soup bases, spread on sandwiches, dissolved in water to marinate tofu in before frying, or spread on fried tofu. It is available in Japanese groceries, health food stores, and co-ops.

This recipe provides your family with a highly nutritious and good-tasting beverage. An 8-ounce glass supplies about 9 grams of protein, slightly more than found in the same amount of cow's milk. Soymilk is low in calories and contains no cholesterol. A pound of soybeans will make a gallon of soymilk and can cost your family less than 15¢ if you buy your beans at a co-op or feed store. (If you buy your beans at a feed store, *be sure they aren't treated with mercury—mercury is poison.*)

Serve soymilk hot or chilled, flavored with various extracts, fruit, carob, or cocoa. It makes a smooth milkshake mixed in a blender with a little oil and flavoring.

Preparation:

Rinse **2½ cups whole soybeans** and soak in **5 cups of water**, following one of the methods described below. After the beans are soaked, transfer to a colander and rinse again.

Soak Method I: Soak rinsed soybeans in a bowl or pot of **cold water** for 8-10 hours or overnight. In hot weather the soaking beans should be kept in the refrigerator to prevent souring. Slightly soured beans will make a thinner milk.

Soak Method II: For quick soaking, pour **boiling water** over rinsed beans and allow to soak 2-4 hours. Beans will double in size and be free of wrinkles when done. They will have a flat, not concave, surface when split in half.

Grinding the Beans:

Method I: Combine in a blender **1 cup soaked soybeans** and **2½ cups water**. You can use either cold water or nearly boiling water in this step. The advantage of using hot water is a slightly milder flavor and a shorter wait for your mixture to come to a boil. Blend the beans at high speed to a fine slurry (about 1 minute). Pour contents into a large heavy pot or double boiler (it won't burn as easily). Repeat blender process until all beans are blended.

Method II: Grind the soaked beans using a hand grain-mill or a food grinder (use the plate with the smallest holes). When using a hand grain-mill, set the grind pretty tight, so that it easily allows a fine but slightly gritty bean paste to pass through the stones. With finely ground beans, more protein will be

released into the milk and the yield of tofu will be higher. However, if the grind is too fine, it will be difficult to strain and will cause a pulpy soymilk. Add the **ground bean paste** to a pot of **13 cups boiling water**.

Cooking the Soymilk:

Cook the soymilk in a 1½-2 gallon heavy-bottom pot or double boiler. Set over a medium-high flame and bring to a boil, stirring occasionally. Watch the pot carefully. When the soymilk first starts to boil, turn down the heat immediately and simmer at a low boil for 20 minutes. It's important to be right there with your pot at this step. Soymilk will foam up and boil over quickly, so watch it carefully. If you use an electric stove, remove the pot from the burner when it comes to a boil while you adjust the heat.

Straining the Soymilk:

Set a cloth-lined colander (thin cotton or nylon) over a pot with at least 1-gallon capacity. After the soymilk is cooked, pour or ladle it into the colander, catching the pulp in the cloth and the milk in the pot below. Twist the cloth

tightly closed. With a wooden spoon or a jar, press on the bag to extract as much milk as possible. To rinse through any milk left in the pulp, re-open the cloth, stir in **2 cups boiling water**, twist and press again. Set pulp aside to be used in cooking (see p.145).

Cooling the Soymilk:

You can drink the soymilk hot or you can cool it by placing the pot in a sink of cold water, replenishing the cold water as necessary. When cooled, transfer into covered containers and refrigerate or freeze. The quicker the soymilk is cooled and the colder it is kept, the longer it will last. It has an approximate shelf life of 4-5 days. If it starts to sour, use it for baking in cakes, biscuits, or bread.

Unlike cow's milk, soymilk contains very few natural sugars. For drinking, most people prefer to add a sweetener, vanilla or cocoa, and a dash of salt. Soymilk can be made thicker or thinner by adjusting the proportion of beans to water in this recipe. Soymilk can be used to replace cow's milk in any recipe . . .

. . . except maybe one.

VANILLA MILKSHAKE

2 cups soymilk	2 Tbsp. oil
1 cup ice	1 tsp. pure vanilla
⅓ cup sugar	1/8 tsp. salt

Combine in a blender until ice is well blended. Serve at once. For a thicker milkshake, blend in an extra cup of ice.

Milkshakes can also be made by whipping ice bean (see pp.104-106) and adding a touch of soymilk to thin it down.

SOY NOG

3 cups soymilk	¼-½ tsp. rum extract
½ cup sugar	pinch nutmeg
1 tsp. pure vanilla	1-2 Tbsp. oil

Combine in blender until smooth and serve hot or cold.

BANANA SMOOTHIE

1 cup soymilk
1 cup ice
3 medium-size bananas
2 Tbsp. honey
dash of salt

Combine ingredients in a blender and blend until smooth. Serve immediately.

BANANA SMOOTHIE # 2

A good smoothie can be made with **frozen bananas** instead of ice. Peel and freeze bananas in a plastic container or plastic bag. Start blending **2 cups soymilk, 2 Tbsp. honey,** and **a dash of salt** in blender and add about **4 small frozen bananas.** Drop in one banana at a time. The soymilk will get thick and frothy and should be served immediately. More honey may be added if you want it sweeter.

VANILLA PUDDING

1 cup sugar	**3 cups soymilk**
¼ cup cornstarch	**¼ cup margarine**
¼ tsp. salt	**2 tsp. vanilla**

Combine sugar, cornstarch and salt in a medium saucepan. Gradually blend in the milk, stirring until smooth. Cover and cook over a low heat, boiling gently for about 5 minutes. Remove from heat, blend in margarine and vanilla. Pour into dessert cups and chill. Top with *Soy "Whipped Cream"* (p.141).

CHOCOLATE PUDDING

Mix together well:

⅓ cup cocoa	**¼ cup cornstarch**
1 cup sugar	(⅓ cup cornstarch
¼ tsp. salt	if making a pie)

Then add **3 cups soymilk,** whipping constantly. Bring this mixture to a boil over medium heat, still whipping constantly, then lower the heat and cover. Let boil gently for 5-10 minutes.

Remove from heat and whip in:

3 Tbsp. margarine
1½ tsp. vanilla

Pour into a bowl or baked pie crust, chill, and serve with *soy "Whipped Cream"* (p.141).

LEMON PIE FILLING

Combine in saucepan:
  1½ cups sugar
  ½ cup + 1 Tbsp. cornstarch
  ¼ tsp. salt

Whisk in **2¼ cups water** (or half water and half soymilk) and bring to a boil over medium heat. Cook 3-5 minutes, stirring often with a whisk. Remove from heat. Stir in **3 Tbsp. margarine** and slowly add **¾ cup fresh** or **reconstituted lemon juice.** Pour into a prebaked **9" pie shell.** Chill. Serve topped with *Tofu "Whipped Cream"* or *Soy "Whipped Cream"* (pp.140,141).

SWEET POTATO PIE FILLING

1½ cups sweet potatoes, peeled,
  cooked, and mashed
2 Tbsp. melted margarine
1¼ cups soymilk

¾ cup sugar	**½ tsp. ginger**
2 Tbsp. sorghum	**¼ tsp. nutmeg**
½ tsp. salt	**¼ tsp. cloves**
1¼ tsp. cinnamon	**4 Tbsp. cornstarch**

Mix all ingredients well with a whisk. Pour into an unbaked **8" pie shell.** Bake at 350° for 1 hour. Cool slightly or chill and serve topped with *Soy "Whipped Cream"* (p.141).

Chocolate and Vanilla Pudding with Bananas

ELIZABETH'S DOUBLE DUTCH CHOCOLATE ICE BEAN

1¾ cups sugar
½ cup cocoa
real good pinch salt
½ tsp. vanilla
¼ cup oil
3 cups soymilk

Put sugar in blender, cocoa on top, and salt and vanilla. Put in half the milk and blend till the cocoa is smooth. Then add the rest of the milk and oil and blend till mixed.

Follow directions for freezing from your hand-crank machine or electric ice cream machine.

VANILLA ICE BEAN

1 cup sugar
3 cups soymilk
1½-2 tsp. pure vanilla
¼ cup oil (more or less, depending on how rich you want it)
a pinch of salt

Blend this in a blender, then add ¾ **tsp. liquid lecithin.** Blend it—be sure to blend it well. Put it in your machine and let 'er crank.

PINEAPPLE SHERBET

1 cup crushed pineapple
2 cups soymilk
2 Tbsp. oil
1/8 cup sugar
¼ tsp. vanilla
dash salt

Blend the fruit with half the soymilk and oil and the rest of the ingredients. When it's smooth, add the rest of the milk and the rest of the oil.

Follow directions for freezing from your hand-crank or electric ice cream machine.

HONEY BANANA ICE BEAN

Blend:

3 cups soymilk   **4-6 Tbsp. oil**
1 large or **2 medium**   **½ cup honey**
  bananas   **dash of salt**

Freeze mix in an ice cream machine.

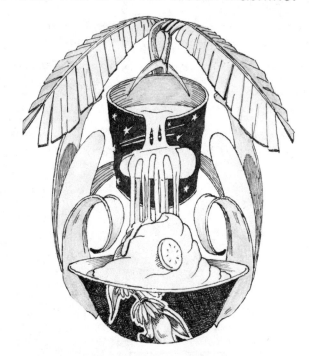

CAROB ICE BEAN

3 cups soymilk   **¼ cup oil**
1 cup sugar   **1 tsp. vanilla**
¾ cup carob   **dash of salt**

Blend 1 cup soymilk, sugar, carob and oil into a smooth paste. Blend in remaining ingredients. Freeze in an ice cream machine.

STRAWBERRY FROGURT

3 cups soy yogurt
1½ cups strawberries
1¼ cups sugar (use ¼ cup less with
   frozen, sweetened strawberries)
dash of salt
¼ cup oil

Blend together and freeze in an ice cream machine.

Ice Bean

ORANGE VANILLA FROGURT

3 cups soy yogurt
1 cup sugar
3 Tbsp. frozen orange juice concentrate
1-2 tsp. vanilla
dash of salt
¼ cup oil

Combine in a blender and freeze in an ice cream machine.

Yogurt can be made from soymilk as well as cow's milk. To make yogurt, place inverted, clean jars in a pot of water. Bring water to a boil and let it boil for at least 2 minutes. Throw in the caps and a clean rubber spatula to be used to stir in the starter later.

Heat the **soymilk** to a boil and hold for 30 seconds, stirring *constantly.* Pour into hot sterile jars. Cover. Let cool to about 110°, or until the jar feels hot to your wrist but does not burn.

Add **2 Tbsp. yogurt** to each quart. (This can be from a good brand of plain cow's milk yogurt to start with, if a commercial yogurt starter isn't available.) Stir briskly with the sterilized spatula, cover and incubate for 2-6 hours at approximately 105°. Yogurt is done if, when you tilt the jar gently, it separates easily and cleanly from the jar sides. Refrigerate. Good plain, salted, or with sweetener and cut up fruit such as bananas or peaches.

For a thicker yogurt, make a thicker soymilk by adding either less water or more beans to the soymilk recipe. A jar of this yogurt can be set aside and used to start an additional batch of yogurt. Use 3-4 Tbsp. of this yogurt per 1 qt. of soymilk.

Yogurt can also be made in a pressure cooker because of its tight-sealing lid. Bring milk to a boil for 30 seconds. Put the lid and jiggler on the pot and set in a sink of cold water to cool. Check it in about 10-15 minutes. Shake the pot a few times to evenly distribute the heat of the soymilk, and remove lid. The soymilk should be fairly hot (about 110°). You can use a sterile candy thermometer. Stir in starter with a sterilized spoon, replace lid and jiggler, and incubate as suggested below.

Incubation:

Put jars or pressure cooker in a warm place such as a gas oven with a pilot light, or a closed insulated picnic cooler box with a drop light turned on inside. Or, put the jars in the oven, turn the oven on to 150° for 3 minutes, then turn it off and let the yogurt incubate, undisturbed, for 2-6 hours.

Yogurt with Peach Slices

For making transfers and larger batches of yogurt:

A good "mother" culture of yogurt can be made by culturing one quart jar of soymilk with a package of freeze-dried starter. From this quart jar you can inoculate 16 gallons of soymilk. About 1 Tbsp. will do a quart and ¼ cup will inoculate 1 gallon. Use your original quart jar to make another quart jar which can be used as your second generation starter. This jar will inoculate another 16 gallons.

Remember to be very clean in order to keep your yogurt from getting contaminated. Keep your hands well washed. Should your yogurt get pink, fizzy or slimy, throw everything out, sterilize all equipment, and start again.

RICHARD'S YOGURT CHEESE

A delicious cheese can be made from **yogurt** by placing the fresh thick curds in a nylon or lightweight cotton cloth. Twist the cloth into a ball and tie with some thin cord. Hang this over a sink or a pot for a few hours. This will make a nice moist cheese. If you want a denser cheese, hang longer or press for a while. This cheese is a basis for cottage cheese, cream cheese, dips, salad dressings, and cheesecakes.

If your yogurt isn't nice and thick so that it will hang into curds easily, you can try heating it some. The heat will help it to curd more and the curds will be firmer and press out easier. The disadvantage with this is that the active yogurt cultures are killed by the heat and the cheese is drier. It makes a nice cheese, though!

YOGURT "COTTAGE CHEESE"

To make "cottage cheese," just sprinkle **salt** over a bowl of moist **yogurt cheese curds.** Serve on a lettuce leaf and garnish with paprika and a sprig of parsley.

YOGURT SOUR CREAM

1 cup moist yogurt cheese
2 Tbsp. oil
4 tsp. fresh lemon juice or **vinegar**
1½ tsp. sugar
¼ tsp. salt

Blend ingredients in a blender till smooth. Pour into a dish and chill.

YOGURT CREAM CHEESE

1 cup moist yogurt cheese
2 Tbsp. oil
1/8 tsp. salt
½ tsp. sugar
½ tsp. soy sauce

Blend ingredients in a blender until smooth. Pour into a dish and chill for an hour or two.

YOGURT CHEESECAKE

3 cups moist yogurt cheese
¼ cup oil
¼ cup margarine
1 cup sugar
¼ tsp. salt
1¼ tsp. vanilla
1 Tbsp. lemon juice (fresh is best)
¼ cup soymilk, yogurt, or **water**
  (if necessary to blend)

Combine above ingredients in a blender and pour into a cheesecake crust (p. 137). Bake at 350° for about ½ hour or until the filling looks set and when you touch the top your finger stays clean.

YOGURT WHIZ

This drink is best made with fresh fruit in season and is a great icy drink for a hot summer day.

1 cup yogurt
1 cup ice
1 cup fresh fruit (strawberries or
  raspberries are good)
2 Tbsp. sugar (more may be added
  depending on type of fruit used)
dash of salt

Combine ingredients in a blender and serve immediately.

TOFU

Tofu has been a staple food for millions of people in Asia for centuries. Tofu contains high quality protein, no cholesterol, is low in calories, and is inexpensive to purchase or make at home.

Because of its smooth texture and ability to absorb and complement other flavors, tofu is one of the most versatile forms of using soybeans. Tofu can be used as fillings in Mexican dishes, in casseroles, or in place of ricotta cheese in any Italian recipe. It makes great sandwiches, spreads, and pizzas. Blended, tofu can be made into dips, sauces, cream pies, or cheesecakes. The recipes in this book are only a sampling of all the dishes that can be made from tofu. Use your imagination to create your own recipes.

There are different types and textures of tofu, and this is good to know when cooking with it or making it. Some tofu contains more water and is softer and silkier. This is the best kind to use for blender products or soft spreads. Other tofu is denser and firmer and is better for slicing, deep frying or crumbling, but doesn't blend as smooth. Techniques for making both kinds of tofu at home are given in the following recipes.

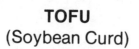

TOFU
(Soybean Curd)

To make tofu, follow the recipe for making soymilk on page 95, changing the proportions to **3 cups water** for every **1 cup soaked soybeans.** After the soymilk is strained and while it's still very hot, prepare the solidifier.

Combine **1 cup warm water** with:

- **1½-2 tsp. nigari,** or
- **1½-2 tsp. epsom salts,** or
- **¼ cup vinegar,** or
- **¼ cup lemon juice.**

Nigari is our preferred solidifier. It is made by removing the sodium and water from sea water. The remaining minerals are the nigari in a crystallized form. Nigari produces a nice firm tofu, more subtle in flavor than tofu made with epsom salts or vinegar, and yields a good amount of protein. It also supplies your body with added minerals, among them potassium, magnesium, and calcium.

Epsom salts (magnesium sulfate) is good for a high yield of tofu and is easy to find in a drug store.

Vinegar or lemon juice usually produces soft curds. However, if boiled for a few minutes they can become quite firm. Vinegar and lemon juice are easy to purchase and add a nice tart flavor to the tofu.

There are different variables to consider that affect the amount of solidifier to add when making tofu. The variety of beans used, the temperature of the soymilk (should be about 185°), the strength of the solidifier, and the method of curding, all affect the final product. After making tofu a few times you'll develop a feel for how much to add and when.

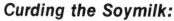

Curding the Soymilk:

While the strained soymilk is fresh and hot, stir slowly with a wooden spoon in a circular motion and pour in half of the solidifying solution. Slowly stir in the opposite direction to create a current that will mix the solidifier in well. Sprinkle a small amount more solidifier (¼ cup) over the top of the soymilk. Cover the pot to retain the heat for proper curding, and allow the milk to set undisturbed for 5 minutes. The tofu will start to form large white curds. If the soymilk is still milky-looking, poke the top few inches gently to activate curding and then gently stir in the rest of the solidifying solution if necessary. Cover pot again and let set a couple more minutes.

The end result here should be large white curds floating in a clear yellow liquid called *whey.* If there is any milky liquid left, stir it gently into the whey to help it curd. If after a minute of stirring there isn't any noticeable difference in curd and whey formation, make up some additional solidifying solution using approximately ½ tsp. nigari or epsom salts, or 1 Tbsp. vinegar dissolved in ¼ cup hot water. Stir it gently into the pot. Always stir gently to prevent breaking up the curds, and only stir the top few inches of the pot. Take pokes to the bottom of the pot in various places to allow any milk trapped between the curds to come up to the top where it will be curded by the whey. When all of the soymilk is formed into curds and there is only clear yellow whey left, the tofu is ready for the pressing box.

If there is a lot of whey and only a few curds it's possible that the solidifier was too strong or was added too fast, or the beans may not have been ground fine enough, resulting in a thin milk and low yield.

Curding Soymilk

Pressing the Tofu:

Set up a tofu press or a colander in the sink and line with nylon tricot or curtain mesh. Set the pot next to it. Using a ladle or measuring cup, and a large tea strainer or colander with small holes, prepare to ladle the curds into the cloth. To do this, set the strainer in the pot and let it fill with whey. Ladle out whey until most of it is out of the pot. This will help the curds form together for a nice solid tofu. After the whey is removed, ladle the curds into the press, cover with the cloth and put on the lid. If using a colander, place a small plate on top of the tofu.

To press the tofu, use a heavy weight that will fit nicely inside the press. A jar of water or a clean heavy rock or brick can be used. Press for 20-30 minutes. For firmer tofu, use a heavier weight or press longer.

Remove the weight and lid. Tofu should be firm to the touch. Fold back the cloth and re-set the lid directly on top of the tofu. Turn the tofu upside down so the tofu is sitting on the lid. Remove press or colander and gently peel off the cloth. The tofu can be set in a sink or bowl of cold water to get cool and firm.

Tofu should be stored in a container of cold water in the refrigerator. Change the water daily to help preserve freshness. If stored properly, it will keep up to a week.

(Clockwise): Tofu in cloth, Soybeans, Soymilk, and a block of Tofu.

Here are a couple of frequently asked questions:

Q. I followed the instructions but my tofu is still milky among the curds. I added a little more solidifier but still nothing. What should I do now?

A. Probably what happened was the soymilk didn't maintain enough heat during the curding process or sat too long between curdings. Set your pot of curds back on the stove and re-heat. As it heats up it will develop into curds and whey. If it still doesn't, add more solidifier.

Q. During my first curding, the soymilk instantly separated into curds and a lot of whey. Is this common?

A. What happened here was that too much solidifier was added during the first curding. This could have been caused by the milk being too thin (maybe the grind wasn't fine enough), in which case the amount of solidifier added was proportionately too strong. It's also possible that the solidifier was too strong. If you're using vinegar, check it out—it comes in different strengths and might need to be diluted.

Here are some good tips for tofu makers:

- The hotter the soymilk is when curded, the firmer the curds will be. If a very firm tofu is desired, the curds may be placed back on the heat and boiled a few minutes.
- For the highest yield of tofu, the curding should be done slowly (in a few stages). This produces large, soft curds and yields a tofu high in water content. This tofu is especially good for blender products and *Soft Scrambled Tofu.*
- Gently stir the top few inches of the soymilk when you're checking the curds and take a few pokes to the bottom of the pot. This helps to activate the curding and can sometimes be done in place of adding more solidifier. The poking also helps to bring up any milk that's trapped between curds at the bottom of the pot.
- Too much solidifier will give the tofu a strong flavor that isn't as appetizing. Tofu should have a subtle flavor.

Whey

Whey is the clear yellow liquid left over when making tofu. Except when epsom salt has been used as a solidifier, the whey can be used in bread or soup stocks. It also makes a good hair rinse.

Whey acts as a natural detergent and will suds easily if stirred. It is good for washing and soaking the pots and cloths used during the tofu-making process.

Care and Maintenance of Press and Cloth

Clean your milk-making equipment and cloth well after each use. A mild soap solution may be used. Cloths can be soaked in bleach water occasionally. Whey can be used to wash your equipment, also. A vegetable brush is a good cleaning tool for your colander, press and cloth.

The pot used for cooking the soymilk is the most difficult piece to clean. A copper or stainless steel scrubber can be used. Also, a metal spatula comes in handy for the preliminary scraping of the film that forms along the sides and bottom of the pot. For easiest cleaning, soak the pot in cold water immediately after using. Keep everything clean as you make your soymilk. The quicker your utensils are washed or rinsed, the easier they are to clean.

DEEP FRIED TOFU

Slice **tofu** into ½-¾" slices or 1" cubes. Soak the pieces in **salt water** or **soy sauce** and drain the excess moisture off by laying them on a cloth or towel. Cover with another cloth and allow to set a few minutes, then deep fry in **hot oil** until golden brown and crispy.

Drain on absorbent paper and dust with **nutritional yeast flakes** ☆ (optional) and **salt.** Deep Fried Tofu is good dipped in tofu dressings and dips, in sandwiches or salads, or as cubes to go with spaghetti (see p.34, *Spaghetti Sauce*).   ☆ See page 58.

Pan Fried Tofu

PAN FRIED TOFU

Slice **tofu** ¼-½" thick. Dip in **soy sauce** (optional) and pan fry in **margarine** or **oil** until golden brown. Pan Fried Tofu is good in sandwiches or cut in cubes and fried with onions and vegetables.

BREADED TOFU

Combine:
   ½ **cup flour**
   ¼ **cup nutritional yeast flakes** ☆ (opt.)
   ½ **tsp. salt**
   dash pepper
   garlic, oregano, basil (opt.)

Slice **tofu** ¼-½" thick. Dip in **soy sauce** (optional) and then in the flour mixture. Fry until golden brown.

BARBEQUE TOFU

Pan fry or deep fry ½-¾" slices of **tofu** (see p.124). Line the bottom of a baking pan with the fried tofu and cover with *Barbeque Sauce* (p.83). Bake at 350° for about 20 minutes. Serve with rice or in a sandwich.

If you are using *Deep Fried Tofu*, you can grill it over charcoals in a barbeque pit while basting with the barbeque sauce.

☆ See page 58.

TOFU POT PIE

Have ready one partially baked **pie shell** (p.128).

Combine in a paper bag:

½ cup flour
2 Tbsp. nutritional yeast flakes ☆ **(opt.)**
1½ tsp. salt
½ tsp. garlic powder

Add **4 cups tofu** cut in ½-¾" cubes and shake.

Saute the cubes in **¼ cup oil** until lightly browned. Then add:

1 cup onions, chopped in large chunks
1 cup celery, chopped
½ cup carrots, chopped
1¼ cups peas, fresh or frozen

Saute until onions are limp, then add:

½ tsp. garlic powder
2 Tbsp. soy sauce

Put this mixture in the partially baked pie shell, cover with *Golden Gravy* (p.63), and mix in gently. Cover with pie crust, poke top crust and bake at 400° for 30 minutes or until top is golden.

☆ See page 58.

TOFU "GRILLED CHEESE" SANDWICHES
Makes 10

Stir **2½ cups** lightly salted, crumbled **tofu** into 1 recipe of *Melty Nutritional Yeast "Cheese"* (p.59). Spread between two slices of **bread**. **Margarine** the outsides and grill. **Tomato** and **onion** slices may be added also before grilling.

This is one of our kids' favorites.

SOFT SCRAMBLED TOFU

Saute some **onions** and add crumbled or mashed **tofu** along with **salt, pepper, nutritional yeast flakes** ☆ (opt.), and **soy sauce** to taste. A little **turmeric** can be added for color. Fry the tofu until browned.

☆ See page 58.

TOFU SPINACH PIE

Saute **1½ cups chopped onions** in ⅓ **cup oil** until browned. Add **2½ cups chopped cooked spinach** and saute for 1-2 minutes more. Have ready, well-mixed in a separate mixing bowl:

3 cups tofu, crumbled and salted

1 tsp. garlic powder

¼ cup nutritional yeast flakes ☆ (opt.)

1 Tbsp. lemon juice

Add onions and spinach to the tofu mixture and mix well. Add **salt** to taste. Place in a partially baked pie crust (recipe below) and cover top with pie crust. Bake at 400° approximately 30 minutes, until crust is golden.

Pie Crust: *Makes two 9" shells*

Mix together in a bowl:

2 cups flour

1 tsp. salt

Work **½ cup margarine** into this with your fingers. Add a **scant ½ cup cold water**, stirring as little as possible to form a ball.

Divide into 2 balls and roll out to 1/8" thickness. Prick the pie shell in the pan with a fork a number of times before baking to prevent bubbles. For a partially baked shell, bake at 400° for approximately 10-15 minutes (till lightly browned on edges).

☆ See page 58.

TOFU NOODLES

Mix well in a large bowl:

4 cups crumbled tofu
6 cups flour
1 Tbsp. salt

Add about **1 cup water** (this will vary depending on how wet your tofu is). It should make a moist dough that will stay together when kneaded. Knead it in the bowl until it holds together enough in a ball to be kneaded on a board. Knead 4-5 minutes on the board to develop the gluten in the flour. The dough should spring back when you poke your finger into it.

Divide the dough into 4 parts. Roll out one part at a time on a floured board to 1/10" thick. Sprinkle flour generously over the dough and fold it over gently into a long roll. Cut noodles ¼" wide using a sharp knife. Fluff the noodles with your fingers to unroll them.

Put into **boiling salted water,** bring back to a boil and boil 3-4 minutes. Drain and run cold water over the noodles to wash out excess starch. Add **margarine, salt** and **pepper** to taste.

This is a good high-protein dish for kids.

TOFU MANICOTTI
(Stuffed Noodles)

Prepare *Manicotti Noodles* (p.131) or use **½ lb. large manicotti noodles.**

Filling:

Saute **1 cup chopped onions** in **3-4 Tbsp. margarine** or **oil.** Add:

> **1½ cups chopped cooked spinach**
> **2½ cups mashed tofu**
> **salt** and **garlic** to taste

Stuff the noodles and place them side by side in a greased baking pan that has a small amount of water in the bottom. Cover with *Tomato Sauce* below:

Tomato Sauce:

2 cups tomato sauce	**1/8 tsp. marjoram**
1 cup water	**1 tsp. salt**
1 tsp. garlic powder	**1 Tbsp. oil**
½ tsp. oregano	**2 tsp. sugar**
1 tsp. basil	

Simmer 20 minutes and pour over the stuffed noodles. Next pour a thin layer of *Melty Nutritional Yeast "Cheese"* (opt.) (p.59) over the top, cover with aluminum foil, and bake at 350° for 20 minutes if using home-made noodles, or 40-45 minutes if using un-cooked, packaged manicotti noodles.

CREPE NOODLES FOR MANICOTTI
Makes approximately 10

2 cups white flour
2¼ cups water
½ tsp. salt, scant

Mix flour, water and salt together into a thin, smooth batter. Use more water if necessary. Pour about ⅓ cup of batter into hot, lightly greased skillet and immediately swirl skillet so the batter spreads out evenly and thinly, like a crepe. When the edge of the noodle curls up a little, flip it over and let it cook for about 10 seconds, then remove. The noodles can be stacked. Fill each crepe with a row of filling, roll, and place in pan, folded side down.

Tofu Manicotti

TOFU SALAD

This recipe can be served as a sandwich spread, or scooped on a piece of lettuce garnished with parsley and tomato slices.

3 cups tofu
¼ cup pickle relish
½ medium onion, chopped fine
2 stalks celery, chopped fine
⅓ cup nutritional yeast flakes ☆ (opt.)
2 tsp. soy sauce
1½ tsp. garlic powder
1½ tsp. salt
pepper, parsley, paprika
¼ cup oil or **½ cup soy salad dressing**

Crumble tofu with fingers into a bowl. Add ingredients as listed and stir in oil or *Soy Salad Dressing* (p.141) at the end. Sprinkle with paprika.

TOFU "COTTAGE CHEESE"

A type of "cottage cheese" can be made by crumbling some **tofu** into a bowl and pouring enough *Soy Yogurt* (p.108) over the tofu to moisten it. Sprinkle with **salt**.

☆ See page 58.

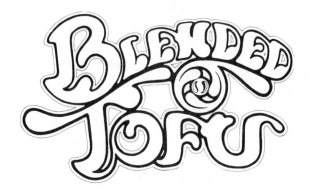

BLENDED TOFU
*For making cheesecakes, cream pies,
dips, dressings, etc.*

When you're blending with tofu it's good to know that all tofu isn't made the same. Different tofu makers incorporate different amounts of water into their product, so that some tofu is softer and silkier and some is slightly denser. This may affect the amount of liquid needed when blending tofu. For this reason, the liquid should be added last or as needed for good blending. A rubber scraper should be used to aid in blending the tofu. Scrape up and down the sides of the blender and fold tofu into the center. Blending small amounts at a time is also useful sometimes, especially when using firm tofu.

The oil content can be adjusted when blending tofu according to how rich a product you want. For dieters, blended tofu is tasty and creamy without any oil at all.

TOFU SALAD DRESSING

1 cup tofu
2-4 Tbsp. oil
1 tsp. salt
4 Tbsp. vinegar
2 Tbsp. sugar
1/8 tsp. garlic powder
pinch of black pepper

Blend ingredients until smooth using a rubber scraper on the sides of the blender. Chill. Serve in place of mayonnaise on burgers or sandwiches, or thin slightly for use on salads.

TOFU TARTAR SAUCE

1 cup tofu
2-4 Tbsp. oil
4 Tbsp. vinegar
2 Tbsp. sugar
¾ tsp. salt
½ cup onion, chopped
1 tsp. mustard (opt.)
1 Tbsp. nutritional yeast flakes ☆ (opt.)

Combine ingredients in a blender and blend until smooth. Use a rubber scraper to aid in blending the tofu.

Pour into a small dish and stir in **¼ cup sweet pickle relish.** Serve on soyburgers, tempeh sandwiches, or tofu sandwiches.

☆ See page 58.

TOFU ONION DIP

2 cups tofu
¼-½ cup oil
¼ cup vinegar
1 tsp. salt
1-2 Tbsp. sugar
½ medium onion, minced
2 tsp. soy sauce
2 tsp. garlic powder
2 Tbsp. nutritional yeast flakes ☆ (opt.)

Combine ingredients in a blender and blend to a creamy consistency. Add a couple tablespoons of liquid if necessary.

Variation: **One package of onion soup mix** can be used in place of fresh onion and spices. Add to first 5 ingredients and blend.

☆ See page 58.   *Tofu Onion Dip*

TOFU CREAM CHEESE

1 cup tofu
2 Tbsp. oil
3 Tbsp. fresh lemon juice or **vinegar**
1 Tbsp. sugar
½ tsp. salt

Combine ingredients in a blender and blend until smooth. Scrape the sides of the blender often with a rubber spatula, pushing the tofu towards the center of the blender. Pour into a dish and chill.

TOFU SOUR CREAM

1 cup tofu
3 Tbsp. oil
3 Tbsp. + 1 tsp. vinegar or **fresh lemon juice**
1 Tbsp. sugar
½ tsp. salt

Blend ingredients until smooth. Scrape the sides of the blender to push tofu into the center. If you want a thinner sour cream, add a little liquid. Pour into a bowl or jar and refrigerate. This is good served on baked potatoes with chopped chives.

TOFU CHEESECAKE

Makes one 9" pie

3 cups tofu
⅓ cup fresh lemon juice
¼ cup oil + ¼ cup margarine,
melted and cooled
1-1¼ cups sugar
¾ tsp. salt
1¼ tsp. vanilla
¼ cup soymilk or **water,** if necessary

Combine ingredients in a blender in order given, adding the liquid at the end only if needed to blend tofu. Mixture should be a fairly thick, creamy consistency. Pour into a partially baked crumb crust (10 minutes at 350°) and bake approximately ½ hour at 350° or until tofu is set in the middle. Tofu cheesecakes may be topped with fruit syrups, fresh strawberries, or fresh cherries.

Crust for Cheesecake

2 cups white flour
½ cup white sugar
¼ tsp. salt
dash cinnamon

2 Tbsp. oil
¼ cup soft mar-
garine, scant
2 Tbsp. water

Mix flour, sugar, salt and cinnamon. Then work in oil and margarine with fingers. Work in water. Pat on bottom and halfway up sides of pan. Partially bake for 10 minutes at 350°. Then fill and bake as above. Be careful, it burns easily.

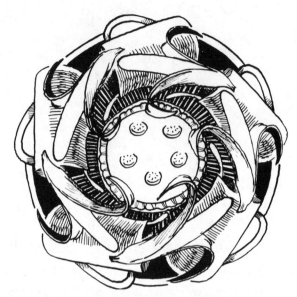

BANANA TOFU CREAM PIE
Makes one 9" pie

Blend in order given:
2-3 ripe bananas
2 tsp. pure vanilla
1 Tbsp. lemon juice
½ cup oil
1 cup sugar
¼ tsp. salt
Add:
2½ cups firm tofu

Blend all ingredients until creamy and smooth. Use a rubber scraper to help blend in the tofu.

Pour the thick creamy blend into a prebaked pie shell and chill for 2-3 hours. Before serving, slice another banana in rounds and decorate the top of the pie.

CHOCOLATE TOFU CREAM PIE
This is a rich one

3 cups tofu
1 cup melted margarine
1½ cups sugar
¾ cup cocoa
2 tsp. vanilla
¼ tsp. salt
½ cup liquid, as needed for blending

Blend ingredients using the liquid to help blend the tofu. Try to blend as thick a cream as possible so it will set nicely when refrigerated. Pour into a **pre-baked pie shell,** top with Soy *"Whipped Cream"* (p.141), and refrigerate a couple of hours.

TOFU "WHIPPED CREAM"

1 cup tofu
4 Tbsp. oil
¼ cup sugar
1 tsp. vanilla
1/8 tsp. salt
½ tsp. lemon juice (optional)
2 Tbsp. soymilk, as needed

Blend the ingredients in the order given, adding the soymilk last only as needed to blend the tofu into a thick cream. Scrape the sides of the blender inward to help blend. The mixture should be thick, but thin enough that it turns by itself in the blender. Chill. Whip the cream with a spoon before serving.

SOY SALAD DRESSING

Makes about one quart

1 cup soymilk
2⅓ cups oil
1 Tbsp. sugar
2 Tbsp. vinegar
1½ tsp. salt

Put cool or cold soymilk in a blender. Pour oil in slowly while blending at high speed. Blend until the mixture gets very thick (about 1 minute). Pour into a bowl and mix in the rest of the ingredients using a rubber spatula. Keep refrigerated.

SOY "WHIPPED CREAM"

¼ cup soymilk
½ cup oil
1 Tbsp. sugar
1 pinch salt
½ tsp. vanilla

Put all the soymilk and half the oil in a blender. At highest speed, blend the milk and oil and slowly pour in the remaining ¼ cup oil. Then blend in the sugar, salt, and vanilla. Chill before serving, if possible.

You'll notice when making or heating soymilk that a layer of skin will form on the top of the milk. This is caused by the oil in the milk rising to the top, and is called *yuba*. Yuba is considered a delicacy in Japan and China where they have small factories dedicated to making it.

The process is simple. Heat soymilk in a pot or shallow pan. When a good layer of yuba forms on the top, cut it around the edges to free it from the pot and slip a chopstick underneath the middle of it through to the other side. Lift up gently.

More than one layer of yuba will form on a pot of milk, so you can get a few sheets by keeping the milk hot and lifting off each layer of yuba as it forms.

Yuba can be scrambled while it's soft and fresh or can be hung to dry until it turns brittle. Dried yuba can be broken up and added to a dish of stir-fried vegetables. (Dried yuba can be stored in the refrigerator.)

Lifting Yuba off the Soymilk

A layer of film will also form on the bottom and sides of the pot when making soymilk. This is also a form of yuba and can be scraped off the pot with a knife or metal spatula. This yuba is usually a tougher consistency and can sometimes be filled with tofu and vegetables, rolled, tucking the ends in, and fried until crispy (like a blintze!).

FRIED YUBA

Place ½ **cup soft yuba** (cut in strips) in a hot frying pan with **1-2 Tbsp. margarine.** Sprinkle with **salt** and **pepper** and **nutritional yeast flakes** ☆ (opt.). Fry till slightly golden, turning once.

☆ See page 58.

SOY "COFFEE"

Roast **soaked soybeans** in a medium (300°) oven on a cookie sheet, one bean deep. Remove from oven when beans are dark brown but not burned. Grind when hot, if possible. Store airtight. Percolate or simmer (don't boil or your coffee will be bitter) in a saucepan for about 5 minutes. Slightly less than 1 Tbsp. of soy coffee grounds per cup of water makes a tasty brew. It tastes a lot like coffee, but it's mellow on your nerves.

SOY "NUTS"

Soak **soybeans** overnight or put them in a pressure cooker with sufficient **water** and **1 Tbsp. oil.** Bring to full pressure and immediately remove from heat, allowing the beans to come down from pressure slowly. (Beans must be well soaked or partially cooked first, or they will be indigestible.) Drain well in a colander or strainer.

Method I: Heat **3 cups oil** to 400° and carefully add **1 cup soaked soybeans.** Fry on full flame for about 7 minutes or until golden brown. Remove beans and drain on paper towels. **Salt** to taste. Make sure the temperature of the oil is up to 400° at the start of each batch.

Method II: Place beans on an oiled cookie sheet, one bean deep, and bake in a moderate oven, turning occasionally, until golden brown, about 30-45 minutes.

Store soy nuts in an airtight container to keep crisp and serve as high-protein snacks.

If you make soymilk, you'll have soy pulp left in the cloth when your milk is done. Although the pulp contains less protein than the milk, the protein is high quality. Soy pulp can be substituted for rice in many recipes. You can make *Soy Pulp Tempeh* out of it (see p.87), or it can be used in baked goods like cake and cookies, where it gives a coconutty flavor when combined with sugar and vanilla extract.

To be easily digested, soy pulp must be cooked until it's soft. Pressure cook the pulp for 20 minutes in **⅓ cup water** for every **1 cup of pulp**; or steam it for 1½ hours.

MARSHA'S SOY PULP GRANOLA
Tastes like coconut wheat germ

2½ cups sugar	**1 tsp. salt**
¾ cup oil	**3 Tbsp. vanilla**

16 cups soy pulp (you need about 12 cups dry soy grits to get this much pulp)

Mix all ingredients well. Then toast in batches in a heavy pan for about 20-30 minutes, or on a cookie sheet in the oven for slightly longer, till very brown and a little crunchy. Watch it carefully and stir often, especially if you're pan-toasting it. It will cook down quite a bit. Spread it out to cool, then store in airtight jars. It will keep a couple of weeks, and even longer if refrigerated.

Good plain, with soymilk and sugar, or mixed with other toasted grains and raisins. Use it as a topping for *ice bean* (pp.104-106).

SOYSAGE

4 cups soy pulp (from making soymilk,
see p.95), or **cooked cracked soybeans**
2 cup whole wheat flour
1 cup wheat germ
¾ cup oil
1¼ cups soymilk (or other liquid)
1 cup nutritional yeast flakes ☆
1½ tsp. fennel seed
1 tsp. black pepper
¼ cup soy sauce
3 tsp. oregano
2 tsp. salt
½ tsp. cayenne
2 Tbsp. brown sugar
2 Tbsp. garlic powder
2 Tbsp. wet mustard
2 tsp. allspice

Mix ingredients. Oil an oven-proof bowl
or empty tin can. Fill it, and cover with tin
foil. Steam on a rack in a covered pot for
1½ hours, or in a pressure cooker in **5 cups
of water** for at least 30 minutes. Let it sit
until cool, then slice it and fry it.

☆ See page 58.

SOYSAGE DOGS

Make *Soft Sandwich Bun* dough (p.171). Let dough rise for 5 minutes in a warm place. Roll out ¼" thick on a well-floured board and cut into 4" strips.

Starting at the side nearest you, place hot-dog shaped *Soysage* (p.146) on the dough. Roll it over once, cut, and pinch edges. Repeat with the rest of the dough. Put dogs almost touching on an oiled cookie sheet and let rise. Bake at 350° for about 20 minutes. Remove from oven and brush tops with **margarine.** Slit open, spread on mustard and stuff with sauerkraut.

SOY PULP COOKIES

2 cups flour
½ tsp. salt
4 tsp. baking powder
2 cups soy pulp (from making soymilk, p.95)

1½ cups sugar
½ cup margarine
½ cup soymilk or **water**
1 tsp. vanilla

Sift together flour, salt and baking powder. Add soy pulp and mix well. Cream sugar and margarine. Add soymilk or water, and dry ingredients alternately to the creamed mixture. Mix well. Add vanilla and mix well. Drop by the spoon on an oiled cookie sheet and bake 20 minutes at 400°

Soy flour is ground up soybeans. Full fat soy flour contains all of the oil in the soybean. Full fat soy flour should be ground fresh or refrigerated, because the oil in it can get a little rancid and give it a poor flavor. Whole soybeans keep well, but once the hull of the bean is broken, the oil will begin to oxidize.

You can grind your own soy flour from whole beans with a small home grain grinder. Some stores or co-ops carry soy flour in the refrigeration section.

Soy flour differs from soy powder in that it is raw and usually contains all of its oil. Low fat soy flour has had most of the oil removed and will keep better without refrigeration.

Soy flour can be added to bread, cookies, and other baked goods. It will substantially increase the protein wherever it is added to the meal. It also helps retain moisture in baked goods.

Soy flour also makes good tofu and milk. It is slightly easier than using whole beans because it eliminates the grinding process. The type of soy flour we prefer is a rather coarse grind, full fat soy flour, which has a texture in between whole wheat flour and cornmeal. Soy powder or fine flour should not be substituted for the soy flour in these recipes, as they absorb water differently and are harder to strain through cloths when cooked.

SOYMILK
Using Soy Flour

4 cups soy flour
12 cups water

Bring water to a boil. Sprinkle soy flour into boiling water, whisking to prevent lumping. Or dip some of the boiling water out of the pot and mix it with the dry soy flour to make a paste. Then pour the paste into the remainder of the boiling water. This method prevents the lumps that sometimes form when dry soy flour is poured directly into the water. Then lower the heat and simmer for 20 minutes, stirring occasionally. Soymilk boils over easily, so pay good attention.

Strain through a clean cloth (nylon tricot is good) placed in a colander or strainer that's set over a pot. Bring the hot milk's temperature down by setting the container in a sink of cold water. Add a **pinch of salt** and **sweeten** to taste. Keep the milk covered and refrigerated.

Here are two different methods of preparing tofu from soy flour, and each method creates a different texture tofu. Farmer's Tofu is a firm tofu great for slicing and frying. The other tofu recipe makes a soft, creamier tofu good for sandwich spreads, pastry fillings, and blender products, yet can also be sliced and fried.

FARMER'S TOFU
Using Soy Flour

This tofu is made by soaking soy flour in water, straining it, and then cooking and curding the milk. A finer ground soy flour will also work with this recipe.

Measure **4 cups of soy flour** into a pot or large mixing bowl and whisk in **14 cups** of **cold** or **warm water,** adding only enough water at first to make a smooth paste, and then whisking in the remaining water. Allow to soak for at least ½ hour.

Set a colander over a pot of at least 2 gallon capacity and line it with a nylon or lightweight cotton cloth. When the mixture has soaked, pour it through the cloth and strain into the pot beneath. A good movement for straining the milk is to take 2 corners of the cloth in your right hand and the other two in your left hand. Raise the right hand higher in the air and then the left (like a seesaw effect). This will help the milk to flow freely from the cloth. After this is done the cloth

can be twisted into a ball and kneaded to remove as much milk as possible. Now place the cloth, with the soy flour wrapped in it, in a bowl and add **2-3 cups additional water**. Knead cloth again under water for a few minutes to remove any additional milk left in the pulp. Squeeze thoroughly. Add milky liquid to the rest of the milk.

Bring the milk to a boil over a medium high flame. Reduce heat. Prepare a solution of **2-3 tsp. nigari** or **¼ cup vinegar** in **1 cup of hot water**. Stir the milk and pour in ½ of the solution. If the milk hasn't formed into curds and whey after a few minutes, stir in more of the solution. Simmer for 20 minutes. Read the tofu instructions on p.116 and follow the same techniques for curding and pressing as described there. Curds should be pressed or hung in a cloth for 10-20 minutes.

Variation: For softer curds, cook the milk, without curding it, for 20 minutes, then remove from heat and curd.

SOFT CREAMY TOFU
Using Soy Flour

Whisk **one part soy flour** into **3 parts boiling water**. Bring to a low boil and cook for 20 minutes. Strain and curd as described in the tofu instructions on p.116.

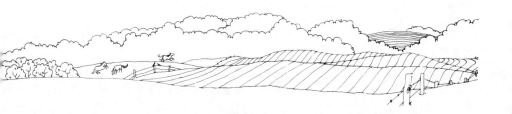

SOY "BUTTER"

¾ **cup soy flour**
¾ **cup water**
1 tsp. salt

Cook in double boiler for 20-30 minutes. Then whip in **1 cup oil** with a whisk or egg beater. Beat until thick and creamy.

SOY "SOUFFLE"

1 cup nutritional yeast flakes
4 cups soy flour
1½ tsp. garlic powder
2½ tsp. salt
½ tsp. turmeric
4 cups water
⅓ cup oil
4 Tbsp. wet mustard

Mix together dry ingredients. Add the wet ingredients and mix. The mixture should be the consistency of ketchup.

Bake in an oiled 9 x 13" pan at 350° for about 45 minutes or until brown on top.

Variations: Add sauteed onions and/or peppers or other vegies to the mixture.

Nutrition Notes: 9 x 13" pan — 150.8 gm. protein; 3½ x 4" piece has 21 gm. of complete protein.

☆ See page 58.

CURDED SOY FLOUR BASE

Bring **12 cups of water** to a rolling boil, then whisk in **3 cups coarse ground soy flour**, sprinkling in a little at a time to prevent lumping. Lower the heat and boil gently for 20-30 minutes. Turn off the heat and gently stir in **½-¾ cup vinegar** or **lemon juice**. When the milk has turned to curds and whey, strain through a clean cheesecloth or nylon tricot cloth placed in a colander. Twist the ends of the cloth to strain all the whey out. This base can be flavored either salty or sweet.

SOY SALAD & SANDWICH SPREAD

To the *Curded Soy Flour Base* above, add:

½ cup margarine   **2 tsp. salt**
1 cup nutritional   **½ tsp. pepper**
yeast flakes ☆

Or, using **5 cups** *Curded Soy Flour Base,* add:

½ large onion, diced
¼ tsp. garlic powder   **¼ tsp. turmeric**
¾ cup nutritional   **¾ cup salad**
yeast flakes ☆ (opt.)   **(soy) oil**
1 cup bread-and-butter pickles, chopped

Mix well. Makes good sandwich spread or dip served with corn chips.

☆ See page 58.

Sprouting is a nice way to farm and grow vegetables in your own home. It's a simple process requiring about 4-5 days of watering and draining and the result is a highly nutritious vegetable rich in vitamins.

Any seed can be sprouted; it's the first step in the life of any plant. Some of the most common and easiest to grow are alfalfa and mung beans. Most sprouts can be eaten raw in salads, sandwiches, or as side dishes.

Materials:
- Seeds—for best prices, purchase seeds in bulk quantities from a food co-op. *Make sure the seeds have not been treated with mercury or other chemicals.*
- Water.
- Container to grow the spouts in—(a) a glass jar with nylon or cheesecloth stretched across the top and secured with a rubber band, or a piece of wire screen cut to fit inside a mason jar ring; or (b) a tray or cake pan (preferably glass or anything rustproof).
- Colander for rinsing seeds.

Basic Steps:

The steps for growing sprouts are the same for all seeds, although some require a longer growth period than others.

1. Rinse your seeds well, about 3-4 times, to remove bacteria and dust.
2. Soak the seeds overnight in lukewarm to cool water to germinate them. If you're sprouting in a jar, soak them in the same jar.
3. Stretch some nylon or cheesecloth over the top of the jar and secure it with a ring or rubber band.
4. Drain by tilting the jar in a sink. If sprouting on a tray, drain the seeds thoroughly in a colander and spread them on the tray.
5. Sprout the seeds in a warm, dark place. Spread the seeds no more than 2 seeds thick for proper growth. If you're using a jar, turn it sideways and shake the seeds so they line the sides of the jar. If you're using a tray, line the bottom with a damp cloth, spread the seeds, and cover with a cheesecloth.
6. Water the seeds whenever they look dry (usually 2-3 times a day). A spray-mister is a good device to use for watering, especially when growing them on a tray. The seeds in the jar can be rinsed under tap water but should be drained thoroughly.

A full-grown alfalfa sprout should be 1" long. Mung beans should be 1½-2" long. Soybeans should be 1½-2½" long.

If the sprouts start to form tiny leaves at the end of the sprout, they are definitely ready to eat.

Sprouts that are kept dark will be yellow. If they are placed in indirect sunlight for a few hours, they will develop chlorophyll and turn green.

Before serving, submerge the sprouts in cold water and agitate slightly. Most of the seed hulls will float to the top where they can be removed. Drain and serve or store in an airtight container or plastic bag in the refrigerator. They will keep refrigerated for a few days.

Alfalfa Sprouts

LAURIE'S STIR-FRIED VEGETABLES WITH TOFU
(Vegetable Chow-Yuk)

(This is my Grandma Lillian's recipe, updated and made vegetarian with the addition of tofu.)

4 Tbsp. salad oil
3 cups firm tofu, cut into 1½" cubes
1 medium onion, sliced
6 stalks celery, cut into 1" slanted pieces
small bunch green onions, cut in
    half lengthwise
2 large bell peppers, cut into strips
½ cup water
⅓ cup soy sauce
2 Tbsp. sugar (opt.)
½ tsp. garlic powder
2 cups mung bean sprouts
½ lb. fresh mushrooms, sliced (opt.)

Heat oil in skillet. Add tofu and cook over a medium low heat until the cubes are browned. Stir occasionally to brown all sides of the cubes.

Add vegies (except sprouts and mushrooms), cover and simmer for 5 minutes, stirring several times. Combine water, soy sauce, sugar and garlic. Mix well and pour over tofu and vegies. Continue cooking at a low heat for another 10-15 minutes. During the last 5 minutes add sprouts and mushrooms. Serve over hot rice.

JANET'S SAUTEED CABBAGE

Saute a **large onion** in **4 Tbsp. oil** until soft. Cut a good-sized **head of cabbage** into eighths, then slice crosswise. Add cabbage to onions along with:

¾ tsp. salt
1 Tbsp. soy sauce
1/8 tsp. pepper
¼ tsp. garlic powder
2 Tbsp. **nutritional yeast flakes** ☆ (opt.)
½ tsp. vinegar
2 Tbsp. oil (opt.)

Cook over medium high heat, stirring often, till cabbage is soft and golden.

☆ See page 58.

Salads

FRENCH CUCUMBER SALAD

2 cucumbers, sliced into rounds
(peeled, too, if not fresh, and then
"scored" with a fork)*
1 medium onion
½ cup apple cider vinegar
1 Tbsp. sugar
½ cup water
½ tsp. salt
¼ tsp. pepper
1 bay leaf

Slice cukes into bowl. Slice onion thin.
Add other ingredients. Toss occasionally, let
sit 1 hour before serving. Chill if possible.

*Scoring—cutting grooves into the cukes—makes the
slices absorb the dressing.*

COLESLAW DRESSING

¼ cup soymilk   **½ cup sugar**
½ cup oil   **½ tsp. salt**
½ cup vinegar   **1 small onion**, chopped

Blend all ingredients together in a blender.
This makes 1 pint of dressing, enough for one
head of cabbage.

JANE'S TRIPLE BEAN SALAD

(Do not overcook the beans. See *Cooking Your Beans,* p.12.)

1 quart cooked green beans, cut in 2" pieces (or 2 cups each green and yellow wax beans)

2 cups cooked, well-drained kidney beans

3 cups cooked, drained garbanzo beans

2 medium onions, cut in half-moons

Optional:

1 stalk celery sliced crosswise, or

1 tsp. celery seed

2 carrots, cut in small strips

Place in shaker jar first:

¼ tsp. garlic powder	**1 Tbsp. sugar**
½ tsp. black pepper	**½ cup vinegar**
1½ tsp. oregano	**½ cup oil**
1 tsp. basil	**¼ cup water**
2 tsp. salt	**½ tsp. marjoram**

First, mix all the herbs, vinegar, oil, etc., in the shaker jar, set aside and let sit while beans cook. Cook and drain all beans, place in a large bowl and toss with the dressing. Let sit refrigerated at least 2 hours before serving, or place in refrigerator overnight. 15 minutes before serving, add sliced raw onions (and other vegetables).

GREEK SALAD

Cut a **tomato** into wedges; peel and slice a **cucumber**; slice ¼ **of an onion** into thin rings.
Combine:

1 Tbsp. oil
1 tsp. vinegar
1½ tsp. sugar
½ tsp. salt
¼ tsp. garlic
1/8 tsp. pepper

Pour over salad.

GUACAMOLE

2-3 ripe medium avocados
1 ripe medium tomato
4 Tbsp. minced onion
¾ tsp. garlic powder
¾ tsp. salt
½ tsp. chili powder
juice of ½ lemon (about 2 Tbsp.)

Peel and mash the avocados. Peel and chop the tomato and add it along with the rest of the ingredients to the avocados. Mix well. Serve with chips or in a sandwich with lettuce and sprouts.

HASH BROWNS

Wash and dry some **potatoes** and grate them up. Put a good amount of **margarine** or **oil** in the middle of a medium hot griddle or skillet and then cover it with a ¼" layer of grated potatoes. Press the potatoes down flat to hold together in a cake. **Salt** and **pepper** to taste and fry with a cover until golden brown. Flip the potatoes over, adding another teaspoon or so of margarine or oil underneath. Fry that side without a lid until golden brown.

You will retain more vitamin C in hash browns if you start with raw potatoes rather than partially cooked ones.

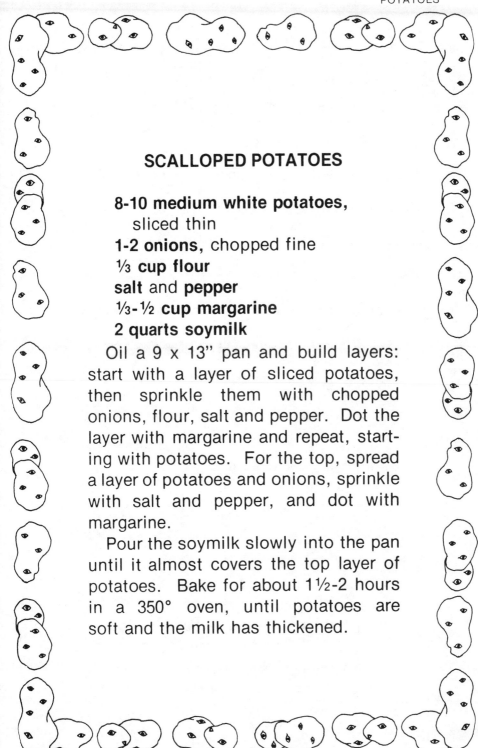

SCALLOPED POTATOES

8-10 medium white potatoes,
sliced thin
1-2 onions, chopped fine
⅓ cup flour
salt and **pepper**
⅓-½ cup margarine
2 quarts soymilk

Oil a 9 x 13" pan and build layers: start with a layer of sliced potatoes, then sprinkle them with chopped onions, flour, salt and pepper. Dot the layer with margarine and repeat, starting with potatoes. For the top, spread a layer of potatoes and onions, sprinkle with salt and pepper, and dot with margarine.

Pour the soymilk slowly into the pan until it almost covers the top layer of potatoes. Bake for about 1½-2 hours in a 350° oven, until potatoes are soft and the milk has thickened.

1. Make sure the edge of the jar has no rough flaws, cracks, chips or nicks. It needs to be smooth so the sealing compound on the lid will stick securely.

2. Clean jar with hot water and soap. Do not use steel brush or pad because it will scratch jar.

3. Sterilize jars, tongs, long wooden spoon, and funnel in boiling water for 2 minutes. Have them hot when ready to fill.

4. Bring sealing lid and screw rims to simmer and keep hot till ready to use.

5. Fill jar. If there are any big air bubbles, poke out with stock end of wooden spoon or plastic spatula.

6. Wipe top edge of jar and side screwing threads spotlessly clean with a clean, damp cloth. This will help make a good seal. Then seal by water bathing or pressure cooking your jars.

Refer to the *Ball Blue Book* for water bathing techniques and additional information.

ELLEN'S HOT TOMATO SALSA
Makes 1½-2 quarts

6-8 cups ripe tomatoes, blanched and peeled, or **2 cups tomato sauce**
2 cups water
2 cups green or **yellow hot wax peppers** or **green chilies** (add a jalapeno pepper if you like it *hot*)

¼ cup onions	**1 tsp. garlic powder**
3-4 tsp. salt	**2 Tbsp. vinegar**

Blanch your tomatoes by dipping them in boiling water for 30-60 seconds (depending on tomatoes' ripeness) in a wire basket or cloth bag. Immerse them in cold water and drain. The skins should come off easily. If not, dunk in boiling water again. After peeling off skins, chop in large pieces and put in saucepan.

Finely chop peppers* and onions and add to tomatoes. Add rest of ingredients and bring to a boil. Simmer for about 45 minutes to an hour. Stir occasionally. If the salsa gets too thick while cooking, add more water. The consistency should be juicy. If it's too watery, cook longer. Tomatoes vary on water content.

You can make this recipe as large as you want. When making a large quantity, you can use a food grinder with a coarse setting for grinding the onions and peppers.

*Hint: Before cutting or working with peppers, oil your hands generously to prevent burning. You can also use rubber or plastic gloves. If you do happen to burn your hands on the pepper juice, take a box of salt and pour generously into both hands. Then gently rub your hands together, making sure you get all parts of the hand. This is an old remedy from Stephen's Aunt Margie, and it works.

MARINATED KOHLRABI

Wash **kohlrabi** and trim fibrous parts off. Cut into sections of about eighths. Steam until they are tender but not so soft that they fall apart. A fork should go into it smoothly. In a hot sterile quart jar, add:

- 1 tsp. salt
- 1 heaping tsp. garlic powder
- 1 heaping tsp. oregano
- ¼ tsp. black pepper

Then pack in the kohlrabi just tight enough so you don't squash it. One **small diced onion** packed in is good. Pack kohlrabi just under first rim. Then add **boiling vinegar** up to ½" under first rim and add enough **vegetable oil**, leaving ¼" head space. They should be well covered. Proceed with canning instructions or eat in one hour.

PICKLED EGGPLANT

Peel and slice **eggplant** crosswise or like french fries. Place in large pot and sprinkle lots of **salt** on them, and place a heavy weight on top. Let sit for a good 2 hours and then squeeze the juice out. This process extracts the bitterness and changes the texture. Next pack in hot, sterile quart jars. Layer spices and onions on eggplant while packing. To each quart, add:

1½ tsp. garlic powder   **¼ tsp. black pepper**
1½ tsp. oregano   **1 onion,** chopped

Pack firmly but not too tightly so that the vinegar will be able to soak in. Fill jar just under the first rim with eggplant. Then pour **boiling vinegar** up to ½" below first rim. Then add **vegetable oil**, leaving ¼" head space. This should well cover the eggplant. Proceed according to canning instructions (p.164) or eat it in an hour.

Fresh ground flour has more vitamins than any pack-aged flour you can buy in a store. If you have your own hand grinder, you can buy wheat by the bushel and grind up however much you need of whatever grade flour you like. If you keep the germ in the flour, you must refrigerate it if you're not going to use it right away.

BASIC BREAD-MAKING TIPS

- If the water is too hot it will kill the yeast. If the water isn't hot enough, the yeast won't grow. Slightly warmer than body temperature is good.

- Any sweetener—sugar, honey, molasses, or white potato water—will feed the yeast and make it grow.

- If you double a recipe, you don't have to double the yeast, although you can. The sweetener makes the yeast grow. Your loaves won't rise quite as much when you don't double the yeast.

- Gluten is what makes the dough stick together, and wheat flour has the most gluten. So if you're adding different kinds of flour—rye, corn, barley, soy—add your wheat flour first, stirring it real good, and then add your other flours last.

- Knead bread dough the same way you knead potters clay. Have it in a lump. Draw a piece from the back of the lump towards you, stretching and folding it over towards the front, and push it back into the lump of dough with the palm of your hand. This is to incorporate air into the dough and to develop the gluten. Shift the lump a little with your other hand, moving it in a continuous circular motion after each kneading stroke. Your lump will become a homogenous ball of dough.

- Sometimes if I'm in a hurry, I'll just make the dough into rolls or a loaf, let it rise only once, and then bake it.

BARBARA'S WHOLE WHEAT BREAD

In a small bowl, mix:

1 cup warm water
2 Tbsp. baking yeast
2 Tbsp. sugar

Stir it once or twice and then let it sit so the yeast can grow a little. In a large bowl mix:

2 cups water
¼ cup sugar
1½ tsp. salt
2 Tbsp. oil

Add the yeast mixture to this and mix well. Add **6 cups unbleached white flour** and stir well for a few minutes to get rid of all the lumps and to develop the gluten. Stir in **4½ cups whole wheat flour.**

Knead it for about 5 minutes or until the texture is even. Put the dough in a bowl and cover it with a wet towel. Put in a warm place to rise till double in size. Punch it down and form dough into two loaves. Let them rise, covered with the towel, in oiled pans, and then bake at 350° until done, about 45 minutes.

CORNELIA'S GOOD WHITE BREAD

Makes 2 loaves

Heat **3 cups water** until quite warm. Put in a large bowl and add **3 Tbsp. sugar** and **1 Tbsp. salt** and stir well. Sprinkle with **3 Tbsp. yeast.**

Let sit away from drafts until foamy, about 5 minutes. Gently stir in **4 cups flour.** Beat lightly to make a wet sponge. Cover and let rise in a warm place until double in bulk, about 20 minutes. Add **2 Tbsp. oil** and beat it down, gradually adding **3 cups flour.**

Turn onto a lightly floured board and knead in **1 cup flour,** until dough is a soft, together ball. Place dough in an oiled bowl and oil the top. Cover and let rise until double in bulk, about ½ hour. Punch down and turn onto a lightly floured board. Knead a few times to get all the air out and shape loaves.

Place in oiled bread pans, cover, and let rise until almost double in bulk (½ hour). Bake for 15 minutes in a preheated 400° oven. Reduce heat to 350°, bake 35 minutes more. It's done if it sounds hollow when tapped on the bottom with your fingernail. For a soft, bright crust, remove from pans, brush all sides with melted **margarine**, and cover with a damp cloth.

To make rolls:

With your thumb and forefinger held in a half circle, press against the ball of dough. Pinch off the resulting bulge and place the rolls, pinched side down, on an oiled cookie sheet 2" apart. Let rise until double in bulk. Bake at 400° till lightly browned.

SOFT SANDWICH BUNS

Makes about 1 dozen

Heat **2 cups soymilk** to scalding. Pour into bowl containing:

¼ cup margarine or **oil**
½ cup sugar
1½ tsp. salt

Combine in a small bowl:

¼ cup lukewarm water
2 Tbsp. yeast
¼ tsp. sugar

Let sit 5 minutes. After the milk has cooled, add the yeast mixture. Then add **1½ cups flour** and beat about 200 times. Let rest for 5-10 minutes. Add **4 cups more flour** and beat well.

After this is added, you will begin to mix with your hands. Depending on the type of flour you're using, add about **1 more cup flour** or enough to produce a consistency of dough that can be turned out onto a floured board. Knead 5 minutes. Put in a well-oiled bowl and let rise for 1 hour. Punch down, and form rolls. Place on oiled cookie sheet. Let rise ½ hour. Bake at 375° for about 20 minutes, or until the bottoms are brown and the tops are beginning to brown. Brush with **margarine** or **oil**.

JANET'S BAGELS

Makes about 30

Dissolve **2 Tbsp. baking yeast** and **6 Tbsp. sugar** in **2 cups warm water.** Add **2 cups gluten flour or unbleached white flour,** beating it in with a whisk. Let rise as a sponge for 10 minutes. Beat in **½ cup oil, 2 tsp. salt,** and about **4 more cups flour** (use a whisk until it gets too thick—then just use a spoon).

Turn dough out on a floured board and knead for about 10 minutes. Add only enough flour on the board to prevent sticking. The dough should be soft but not sticky. Roll lumps of dough between your hand and the worktable into rolls ¾ x 8". Take one end of a roll and wrap around your first two fingers into bagel shape, sealing the two ends by rolling them together between your fingers and the worktable to make a smooth seam. Let rise 5 minutes on a well-floured board.

Have ready a 4-quart pot two-thirds full of **boiling water.** Add **⅓ cup sugar.** Drop 4 or 5 bagels into the rapidly boiling water, risen side down, and put on a lid. Boil 30 seconds on one side, then 30 seconds on the other, keeping a rapid boil all the time. Remove bagles with a slotted spatula and place about ½" apart on a well-oiled cookie sheet. Bake at 375° for 25-30 minutes, or till golden brown.

RYE BREAD

1½ cups warm water
2 Tbsp. active dry yeast

Sprinkle yeast over the warm water. Let sit for 10 minutes until dissolved. Then add:

¼ cup molasses or **sugar**
3 tsp. salt
3 cups all-purpose flour
3 cups rye flour
1 Tbsp. caraway seeds
1 small onion, chopped (opt.)

Knead well, adding more flour if necessary. Let rise in a warm place until doubled, then punch down. Separate into 2 parts and shape into loaves. Place in oiled bread pans and let rise again till doubled. Bake at 375-400° for 30-45 minutes.

HIGH-PROTEIN SOY BREAD
Makes 2 loaves

Scald **3 cups soymilk.** Cool to warm, then sprinkle over milk:

2 Tbsp. baking yeast
¼ cup oil or **melted margarine**
1 Tbsp. salt
2 Tbsp. honey or **sugar**

Let sit for 10 minutes and let yeast foam. Then beat in **4 cups white flour.** Next beat in **2 cups soy flour.** Then knead in **3 more cups white flour.**

Knead for about 10 minutes or until it is a smooth ball. Let rise till double. Punch down and shape into two loaves. Brush tops with **oil** or **melted margarine.** Cover and let rise till almost double. Then bake at 350° for about 45 minutes or until golden brown.

Nutrition Notes: This bread is high in protein of a good quality. Wheat and wheat bread don't have enough of the essential amino acid lysine to be a high quality protein. Alone, the protein of wheat and wheat bread is 41% efficient (available to the body). In combination with soymilk and soy flour, the protein of bread is 87% efficient.

There are 6.9 gm. of total protein in each slice of this bread (15 slices per loaf). At 87% efficiency, that is 6 gm. of complete protein per slice. Most other bread, whole wheat or white, contains 2 to 2.4 gm. of total protein per slice, and it is only 41% efficient.

QUICK FRENCH BREAD
(*One of our kids' favorites*)

3½ cups warm water   1 Tbsp. salt
2 Tbsp. margarine   2 Tbsp. baking yeast
3 Tbsp. sugar   9 cups white flour

Mix water, margarine, sugar, and salt. Sprinkle yeast on top and let rest for 10 minutes. Whip in 7 cups of flour, then beat in the rest with a spoon. Do not knead. Let rise until double. Punch down and separate into two balls. Flatten each ball into a rectangular shape, then roll into a long loaf. Let them rise on an oiled cookie sheet until almost double. Put a pan of boiling water on the bottom of a 400° oven and bake. After 15 minutes, reduce heat to 350° for about 30 minutes. Five minutes before bread is done, brush loaves with **melted margarine.**

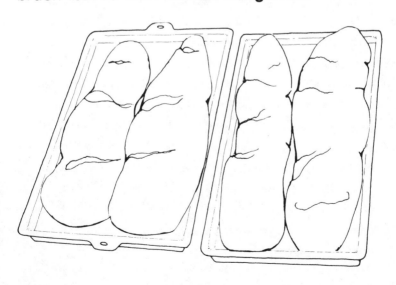

SERGE'S FRENCH BREAD

Makes 3 small loaves

8½ cups flour
2½ cups cold water
50 mg. ascorbic acid
   (vitamin C)
¼ cup warm water
2-3 Tbsp. yeast
2 tsp. sugar
2 tsp. salt

Mix flour, water and vitamin C in a bowl. Knead for 15 minutes. Dissolve yeast and sugar in warm water. Knead yeast mixture into dough till well mixed.

Knead salt into the dough for 10 minutes. Let bread rise 20 minutes. Preheat oven to 400° and put a pan of boiling water at the bottom.

Shape bread into loaves. Make 3 slits on top of each loaf, 3" long and not very deep. Bake till brown, about 30 minutes. Brush on **margarine.**

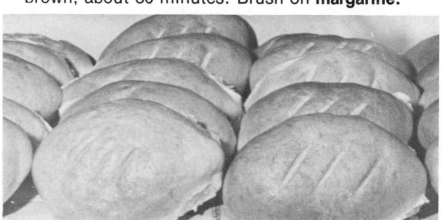

CROISSANTS

2 tsp. baking yeast   **5-6 cups flour**
2 cups warm water   **2 tsp. salt**
¾-1 cup sugar   **1 lb. cold margarine**

Dissolve yeast in ¼ cup warm water and 2 tsp. sugar.

Mix half the flour, remainder of water, sugar, and salt together. Add yeast mixture and enough flour to make a kneadable dough. Knead till soft but not wet. Let rest 5-10 minutes.

Sprinkle flour over the worktable. Flatten the dough—pull gently, but don't tear or roll out—to about 2" thick. Dab the margarine all over the dough with fingers.

Fold the dough into thirds (left side to middle, then right side on top). Roll to ½" thick. Re-roll and re-fold 2 more times, letting the dough rest 5 minutes each time between rollings.

Preheat oven to 350°. Roll the dough flat and cut into 6" bands with a knife. Cut triangles by making diagonal incisions. Pull and stretch the triangles and make a slit in the middle of each one's base. Then roll, starting from the base up to the point.

Put on a cookie sheet and let rise 5-10 minutes. Brush on margarine. Bake ½ hour or until golden brown.

BREADSTICKS

Makes about 3 dozen

Mix together **2 Tbsp. sugar** and **2 Tbsp. baking yeast.** Dissolve it in **1 cup warm water.** Stir a little, and let stand in a warm place for 10-15 minutes until risen and foamy. Then whisk in **¼ cup oil.**

Meanwhile, sift together and mix well in another bowl:

3 cups white flour
1½ tsp. salt
4 Tbsp. nutritional yeast flakes ☆
   (for "cheesy" breadsticks)
½ tsp. garlic powder
pinch black pepper

Add this, small amounts at a time, with a whisk, to the first mixture, alternating with pieces of **1 tiny onion,** diced very small. Then continue to mix it with a spoon till it's smooth. Knead it for a while, just till it's a nice soft ball. Roll out sticks of pencil thickness and roll each in some **poppy seeds.** Place close together on oiled cookie sheets and let stand in a warm place till they look bigger. Bake at 400° for about 10-15 minutes or till golden brown on both sides—they get turned over once. Watch them carefully—they cook fast, and get crunchy as they cool. Good hot!

☆ See page 58.

JANIE'S HOME-COOKED BISCUITS

6 cups flour
1½ tsp. salt
5 tsp. baking powder
2⅓ cups soymilk
⅓ cup oil

Sift the dry ingredients. You can have any combination, such as whole wheat/white, white/buckwheat, whole wheat/buckwheat, or all white.

Make a well in the middle and add liquid (sour milk is good), then oil. Stir just enough to moisten, then turn on to well-floured board and knead a little. Roll to ¼-½" thick, depending on how high you like them. Cut with 2" diameter cutter—tin cans with holes cut in the bottom work good. (The bigger you cut them, the less they rise.) Place them real close together on a cookie sheet—don't leave hardly any space between them and bake in a 450° oven for whole wheat, 500° for white and buckwheat. Bake 10-15 minutes, depending on your oven, and look on the bottom to see if done (if they're browned good). You don't have to oil the pan but sometimes some margarine in the pan makes nice crusty biscuits.

SCONES

Makes about 12

2 cups white flour	**4 Tbsp. margarine**
2 tsp. baking powder	**½ cup raisins** (opt.)
¼ cup sugar	**⅔ cup soymilk**
½ tsp. salt	(approximately)

Sift all dry ingredients together. Rub margarine into them with your fingers. Add raisins and enough soymilk for a soft dough. Roll out on a floured board about ½" thick and cut into large rounds or triangles. Bake on an oiled cookie sheet at 475° for 10-12 minutes. Good hot, cold, or reheated.

SOPAPILLAS
"Little Pillows"
(*Fried Bread*)

Dissolve **2 Tbsp. yeast** in **2 cups lukewarm water.** Add **4 tsp. sugar.** Let sit in warm area until the mixture foams, about 10 minutes.

Stir in **2 cups flour** and let mixture rise in warm area for another 10 minutes. Add **2 tsp. salt** and about **4 cups flour**. Knead well and let rise in a lightly oiled bowl and cover with a towel. Roll out to 1/8" thick. Cut into diamond or triangular shapes. Let rise 15 minutes. Deep fry until golden brown. They'll be hollow and can be filled with jam and rolled in sugar, filled with mashed beans, or eaten plain with margarine.

BLINTZES

Combine:

1 cup white flour   **1 Tbsp. sugar**
¼ cup oat flour   **1 tsp. baking powder**
½ tsp. salt

Whisk in **4 cups cold water.** Pour 1/8-1/4 cup batter in a hot, lightly oiled frying pan and immediately tilt the pan to spread the batter evenly over the surface of the pan in about 6" circles. They should be real thin like crepes. Cook only on one side till the top side is dry and has bubbles on it. Stack the blintzes inside a folded cloth.

Filling:

2 cups pressed tofu
6 Tbsp. margarine, melted
½ cup soy sour cream or **blended tofu**
6 Tbsp. sugar   ½ tsp. salt

Place 3 Tbsp. filling in the middle of the cooked side of each blintze. Fold the two ends toward the middle, then fold the remaining sides over each other. Place on a cookie sheet with folded side down. When ready to serve, fry each blintze in **margarine** till crisp and golden.

Serve with *Tofu Sour Cream* (p.136) or fruit sauce, or serve plain.

A high protein cold cereal
Makes 8 cups

Mix together:

3 cups rolled oats
1 cup wheat germ
1 cup sunflower seeds, lightly toasted
¾ cup sesame seeds, lightly toasted
¼ cup soy flour or **powder**
1 cup brown sugar, mixed in
　　½ cup water
½ cup oil
1 tsp. salt
1 Tbsp. vanilla

Toast in a 350° oven on 2 cookie sheets for about 20 minutes or until golden. Turn often with a spatula so it browns evenly. Store airtight and it'll keep.

Nutrition Notes: There are 14.6 gm. of protein per cup of Granola. 82% of this protein is complete. ¾ cup of Granola and ½ cup of soymilk provides 15 gm. of complete protein.

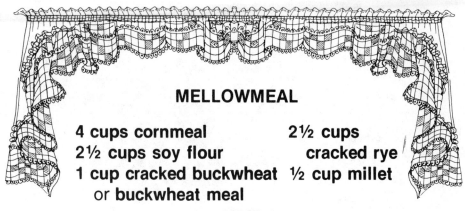

MELLOWMEAL

4 cups cornmeal   2½ cups
2½ cups soy flour   cracked rye
1 cup cracked buckwheat   ½ cup millet
   or buckwheat meal

FARMOLA

2 cups cracked wheat   1 cup cornmeal
   or cream of wheat   1 cup soy flour
1 cup cracked rye

Farmola and Mellowmeal are balanced high-protein breakfast cereals. Both must be thoroughly cooked to make the soy flour and grain digestible. Combine the ingredients well and store in airtight containers.

Whisk 1 part of either cereal into **3 parts salted boiling water.** Stir the cereal constantly while it is first thickening. Then reduce heat and cook for a good 25 minutes, stirring often. Serve hot with soymilk, sugar, sorghum, molasses, margarine, or just plain with salt.

Variation: Toast cereal in a cast iron skillet over medium heat, stirring constantly with a wooden spoon, until grains are browned and have a nutlike aroma. Then cook as above.

Nutrition Notes: There are 20.8 gm. of protein per cup of uncooked Mellowmeal; 95% of this protein is complete. There are 26 gm. of protein per cup of uncooked Farmola; 75% of this protein is complete.

LIGHT AND FLUFFY BRAN MUFFINS

2 cups flour
1½ cups bran or **wheat germ**
½ tsp. salt and **1½ tsp. soda**
2 cups sour soymilk or **yogurt** (see
    pages 95 and 108)
½ cup sorghum or **molasses**
¼ cup oil or **melted margarine**
½ cup raisins (optional)

Sift dry ingredients together and make a well in the middle. Pour in all the liquid ingredients and raisins. Mix together just until everything is moistened, then bake in oiled muffin tins at 450° for 20-25 minutes.

FRENCH TOAST

Mix together with a whisk:

1 cup soymilk or **water**
2 Tbsp. nutritional
    yeast flakes ☆

2 Tbsp. flour
2 tsp. sugar
½ tsp. salt

Dip **slices of bread** one at a time into the mixture until it soaks through but is not soggy. Then fry the slices in **margarine** over medium heat until golden brown and crispy on both sides. Serve hot with cinnamon and sugar or syrup.
☆ See page 58.

PANCAKES

Sift together:
- **1¼ cups flour**
- **2 Tbsp. sugar**
- **2 tsp. baking powder**
- **½ tsp. salt**

Mix together:
- **2 Tbsp. oil**
- **1¼ cups water** or
- **½ cup soymilk**
- **+ ¾ cup water**

Make a hole in the center of the dry ingredients. Pour the wet mixture into the dry and mix with a wooden spoon only until ingredients are blended. The batter should be somewhat lumpy, which makes the cakes light. If you beat the batter smooth, the pancakes will be tough.

You can try replacing 2 Tbsp. of flour with 2 Tbsp. of cornmeal when mixing the dry ingredients. If you use whole wheat flour instead of white, the batter may need more liquid. It should be thin enough to pour.

Heat your griddle over a medium high flame. It's hot enough when water dropped on it turns to beads and bounces across the griddle. Then oil griddle slightly. Pour cakes and flip them when tops bubble up. You may need to lower the flame a little to keep pancakes from burning, but the higher the flame, the lighter the pancakes.

Variation: Add **1 cup well-mashed tofu** to batter.

OLD-TIME BUCKWHEAT CAKES
Makes about 36, 6" in diameter

1 cake or 1 Tbsp. dry yeast
½ cup lukewarm water
2 cups cold water
1 cup flour, white or whole wheat
   (white's best)
2 cups buckwheat flour
1½ tsp. salt
1 Tbsp. molasses
1 tsp. soda
½ cup hot water
4 Tbsp. margarine

Dissolve yeast in lukewarm water. Then add cold water. Sift flour once before measuring. Then sift flour, buckwheat flour and salt together. Blend yeast mixture into the flour mixture. Beat vigorously until the batter is smooth. Cover and let stand overnight.

In the morning, blend in molasses, soda dissolved in ½ cup hot water and 4 Tbsp. melted margarine. Let stand at room temperature for 30 minutes. Drop mixture from tip of spoon onto lightly oiled hot griddle. Cook on one side. When puffed full of bubbles and cooked on edges, turn and cook on other side. Do not mash down.

Note: To use batter as a starter for another batch of buckwheat cakes, save out 1 cup of batter (before adding molasses and soda), add 1 cup of cold water, cover and place in refrigerator until the night before you wish to use it. Pour off water which has risen to the top of batter. Blend in same amount of flour, buckwheat flour and salt as in original recipe. Add 2½ cups cold water, cover and let stand overnight. In the morning, follow directions for adding soda and molasses as in the original recipe.

Variation: This recipe can also be used for making white flour or whole wheat flour pancakes.

MARNA'S GOOD GRIDDLE CAKES

Sift together:
2 cups buckwheat flour
2 cups cornmeal
1½ tsp. salt
1 Tbsp. baking powder
2 Tbsp. sugar (opt.)
Add to dry ingredients:
about 2 cups soymilk or water
1 Tbsp. melted margarine

Mix together—don't worry about stirring out all the lumps. Just add enough until you have a batter than can be easily managed on the griddle. Your griddle is ready to fry when a few drops of water dance across the surface.

Serve them hot with margarine and syrup, or spread with jelly and roll 'em up.

DANISH PASTRY

Cream **1 cup margarine** and **1 cup flour** until well blended. Chill for 30-45 minutes if possible. Dissolve **2 Tbsp. yeast** in **2 cups soymilk** that has been scalded and cooled, or 2 cups lukewarm water. Add **2 Tbsp. sugar.** Let rise in a warm area for 10 minutes.

Then add ½ **tsp. salt,** ½ **tsp. ground carda-mom,** and ½ **tsp. lemon juice.** Stir in **2 cups flour**. Beat until smooth and elastic. Let rise in a warm place for 20 minutes, then beat in ⅓ **cup sugar** and **3½ cups flour.**

Turn out on a lightly floured board and knead until firm. Roll dough into ½" thick rectangle. Place margarine-flour mixture on half of the dough. Fold the other half over the margarine mixture to encase it. Pound lightly. Fold the right-hand third of the dough over the center third. Then fold the left-hand third over the center. Then roll out the dough until about 1" thick. Fold dough

again. Roll. Repeat this rolling and folding 4 more times. Roll into 3 rectangles, the size of cookie sheets and about ½" thick. Place rectangles of dough on oiled cookie sheets.

Spoon on filling (sweetened **tofu** or *Curded Soy Flour Base,* pp.116 and 153, or dried or partially cooked fresh fruit) in a strip down the center third of the dough. With a sharp knife, cut slits in the dough about 1" apart, from the filling out to the edges of the dough (see drawings below). "Braid" the strips of dough over the filled center strip, alternately (see below). Let rise until doubled, from 20 to 60 minutes.

Bake at 375° for 20-30 minutes. Brush with **margarine** when you remove it from the oven. Top with *"Butter Cream" Frosting* (p.190).

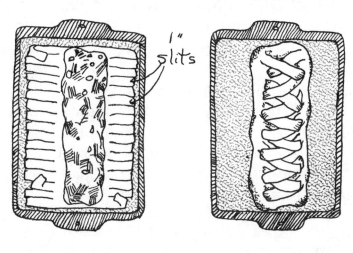

1" slits

CINNAMON ROLLS

Make *Soft Sandwich Buns* recipe (p.171) and let rise ½ hour. Divide dough in half and roll each one into a rectangle 1/8-1/4" thick, keeping enough flour underneath to prevent sticking. Let dough rest 5 minutes, then spread generously with **margarine.** Sprinkle with **2 cups sugar, 2 Tbsp. cinnamon, raisins** (opt.), and **chopped nuts** (opt.). Roll the dough up like a jelly roll, then pinch to seal. Slice off 1" rolls and place almost touching on a margarined cookie sheet. Let rise covered with a damp cloth until light. Bake at 350° for about 20 minutes. Serve warm or glaze with *"Butter Cream" Frosting,* below.

"BUTTER CREAM" FROSTING

Mix **2 cups sugar** with **1 cup water** in a saucepan. Bring to a boil and boil at a moderate heat for 20-30 minutes. The syrup is done when it forms a long, smooth thread when dropped from the end of a spoon. Remove from heat. Cool 30 minutes or until lukewarm. Do not stir from the time you put the syrup on the heat until after it cools. When cool, beat in **1-2 Tbsp. margarine** and a **dash of salt.** Add ½ **tsp. vanilla.**

Variation: Omit vanilla and use ½ **tsp. maple flavoring,** or **2 tsp. instant grain coffee** or **2 tsp. cocoa** dissolved in **1 Tbsp. hot water.**

COFFEE CAKE

2¾ cups flour	1 tsp. cinnamon
1 cup sugar + ½ cup	¾ tsp. nutmeg
brown sugar	½ tsp. cloves
or 1¼ cups sugar	½ tsp. allspice

Sift together above ingredients, then cut in **1 cup margarine.** Set aside 1 cup of mixture for topping.

Add to the rest:

- 1¼ **cups soymilk**
- ¼ **tsp. salt**
- 3 **tsp. baking powder**
- ½ **cup raisins** (opt.)
- ½ **cup chopped walnuts** (opt.)

Beat with a whisk, then pour into lightly oiled and floured 8 x 8" pan. Sprinkle with topping. Bake at 350° for 40-45 minutes, or until knife comes out clean.

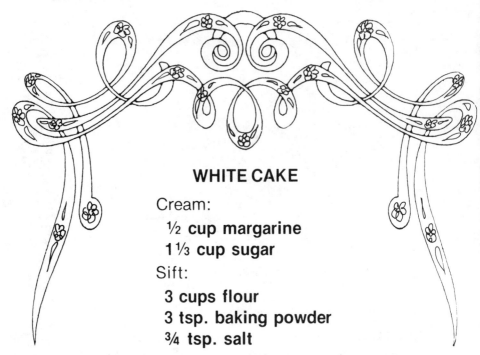

WHITE CAKE

Cream:
  ½ cup margarine
  1⅓ cup sugar
Sift:
  3 cups flour
  3 tsp. baking powder
  ¾ tsp. salt

Mix dry ingredients into creamed mixture alternately with **2 cups liquid** (soymilk or water). Add **1 Tbsp. vanilla.** Beat 2 minutes. Bake in a 9 x 13" pan at 350° for 30 minutes.

Variation: The liquid can be replaced with **2 cups soy yogurt** (p.108) or **whey** (from making tofu, p.116); replace baking powder with **1½ tsp. baking powder** and **½ tsp. baking soda.** Bake as above.

For Marble Cake:

Pour ⅔ of the *White Cake* batter into cake pan. Dissolve ¼ **cup cocoa** in **4 Tbsp. melted margarine** (slightly cooled) and beat until smooth. Add to the remaining ⅓ batter, along with ⅓ **cup sugar.** Beat till smooth. Spoon the chocolate cake batter on top of white batter in pan and swirl with a knife or spatula. Bake as for *White Cake.*

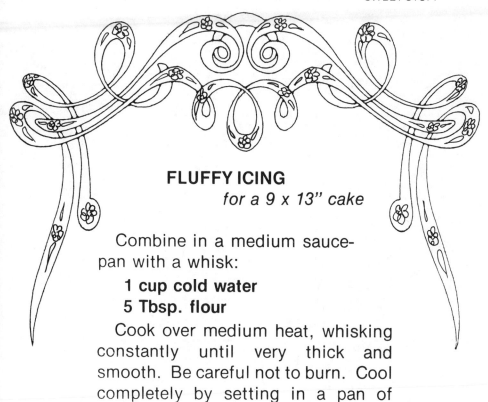

FLUFFY ICING
for a 9 x 13" cake

Combine in a medium saucepan with a whisk:

1 cup cold water
5 Tbsp. flour

Cook over medium heat, whisking constantly until very thick and smooth. Be careful not to burn. Cool completely by setting in a pan of cold water.

Cream until sandy:

1 cup sugar
3-6 Tbsp. margarine
1 tsp. vanilla
pinch of salt
3 Tbsp. cocoa (opt.)

Whip the creamed mixture into the cool flour mixture until well blended and fluffy, then spread on the cake.

If the frosting separates, reheat it while whipping constantly, then refrigerate until cool.

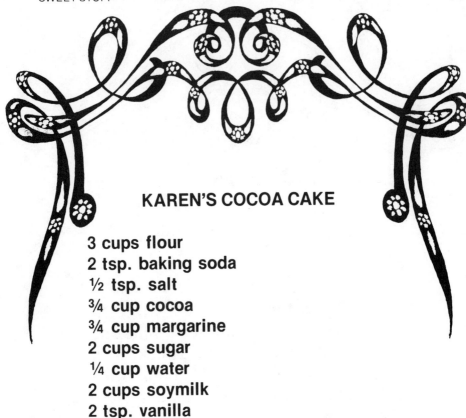

KAREN'S COCOA CAKE

3 cups flour
2 tsp. baking soda
½ tsp. salt
¾ cup cocoa
¾ cup margarine
2 cups sugar
¼ cup water
2 cups soymilk
2 tsp. vanilla

Sift together the flour, soda, salt and cocoa. Set this aside while you cream the margarine. Gradually cream in the sugar. Add the water and beat well.

Add the flour mixture alternately with the milk. Add vanilla and beat well.

Oil and flour a 9 x 13" pan. Pour in the batter. Bake at 350° for about 45 minutes or until a toothpick comes out clean when you poke the center.

ONE MINUTE
FUDGE FROSTING

for a 9 x 13" cake

Mix together in a saucepan:

3 cups sugar
½ cup water
pinch salt
½ cup margarine
6 Tbsp. cocoa
¼ tsp. cream of tartar

Place pan over *low* heat—*important* to prevent sugar from crystallizing. Stir it as it starts to melt, but not after that. Bring to a boil. When entire top of fudge is boiling all over, time for exactly one minute, then remove from heat without jostling. Let it cool (you can put it in a pan of cold water). When it's cool, start beating the fudge. Add **2 tsp. vanilla.** Beat until frosting thickens, and pour and spread on cooled cake. Let set. Serve.

MISS DORSA'S MOLASSES TAFFY

Makes 50 large pieces

⅔ cup molasses
or **sorghum**　　　**1 cup sugar**
3 Tbsp. margarine　**⅔ cup water**

Place ingredients in a medium-size saucepan and cook over medium heat, stirring occasionally. Boil the candy until it reaches the crack stage. Start testing the syrup when the boiling bubbles become deeply concave. When a string of the boiling syrup is dropped into cold water, it should break with a brittle crack. Have a lightly oiled platter ready to pour the candy onto when it reaches the crack stage. You may have to test the boiling syrup several times. Change the water for each test.

When it reaches the crack stage, remove from heat immediately and pour onto the prepared platter. Let it cool just long enough to be able to pick it up and pull it without burning your fingers. It should still be fairly warm and hold together in one piece. Oil your fingers and start pulling the taffy, using just your fingertips and holding it very lightly to allow maximum aeration. It is the air added while the taffy is being pulled that turns it from a dark molasses color to a light golden color. The taffy is done when it gets light and golden and too hard to pull smoothly and rapidly, usually in 10-15 minutes of pulling.

At this point stretch it out into a long even rope and lay it out on a lightly oiled cookie sheet to finish cooling. Cool 10-15 minutes or until the taffy breaks evenly when held in the palm of your hand and struck sharply with the handle of a knife. This may take some practice. Hold the strand of taffy so your hand forms a hollow beneath where you strike with the knife handle. If taffy is undercooked it will be too soft to break and may be cut into bite-size pieces.

BROWNIES

Mix ⅓ **cup flour** with **1 cup water**. Cook until thick and cool completely.

Melt ½ **cup margarine**. Add ⅔ **cup cocoa** and stir until smooth. Cool.

Beat **2 cups sugar, ½ tsp. salt,** and **1 tsp. vanilla** into the cooled flour mixture, then add cocoa mixture.

Mix together **2 cups flour** and **2½ tsp. baking powder** and add to above ingredients. Bake in a 10" square pan at 350° for 35 minutes or until an inserted knife comes out clean. This recipe makes a cakier brownie.

Variation: For fudge brownies, use ¾ **cup cocoa** and decrease the flour mixture to **1½ cups flour** and **2 tsp. baking powder**.

BREAD PUDDING

Serves 4-6

Mix together well:

3½ cups soymilk
⅔ cup sugar
½ tsp. salt
1 Tbsp. vanilla
1 tsp. cinnamon

Pour this over **4 cups of old bread** broken up into bite-size pieces in a square baking pan. Dot the top with ¼ **cup margarine.** Bake for 20 minutes at 350°.

LOUISE'S GINGERBREAD

Makes one 8 x 8" pan

1 cup sorghum or **molasses**
½ cup melted margarine or **oil**
2 tsp. ginger
2 cups flour
1 tsp. salt
1 tsp. soda
   in **1 cup hot water**

Beat together molasses and margarine, then beat in flour, ginger and salt. Beat in soda water about ⅓ cup at a time, till mixture is smooth. Bake at 350° for 35-40 minutes.

HONEYCAKE

Makes one 9" round pan

1 cup honey
¼ cup water
2 cups rye flour
1 tsp. cinnamon
½ tsp. allspice
¼ tsp. mace
2 tsp. baking powder
½ cup chopped nuts

Blend in honey and water, then beat in dry ingredients and blend in nuts. Bake at 350° with a pan of boiling water on the bottom of the oven for about 40 minutes.

Let the cake age in plastic or a tin box for a few days before eating.

APPLESAUCE CAKE

½ **cup oil**
1 ½ **cups sugar**
1 ½ **cups unsweetened applesauce**
2 **cups white flour**
½ **tsp. salt**
1 ½ **tsp. baking soda**
1 **tsp. cinnamon**
   or ¼ **tsp. ginger** + 1/8 **tsp. cloves**
   or ½ **tsp. allspice** + 1/8 **tsp. nutmeg**

Mix oil and sugar well, add applesauce, and mix in the dry ingredients. Beat until smooth. Pour into an oiled and floured 8" cake pan or angel food cake pan and bake at 350° for 45-50 minutes, slightly longer in a loaf pan. This cake is even better the next day.

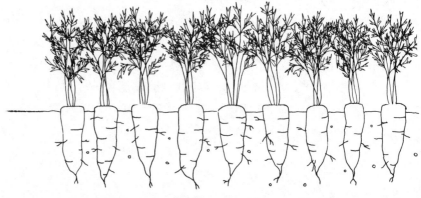

CARROT CAKE

Preheat oven to 350°.

1 cup salad oil
1 cup white sugar + 1 cup brown sugar
   or 2 cups brown sugar
1½ cups water or **soymilk**
4 cups unbleached white flour
2 tsp. baking powder
2 tsp. baking soda
1 tsp. salt
1½ tsp. cinnamon
½ tsp. allspice
3 cups grated raw carrots
1 cup chopped nuts (opt.)
½ cup raisins (opt.)

Blend oil and sugar, add water and beat. Sift the flour with remaining ingredients and add to sugar mixture. Add carrots and nuts and mix well. Bake in 3 oiled and floured layer pans or one 9 x 13" cake pan at 350° for 35-40 minutes. (Baking time may be less if using small round pans.)

BANANA BREAD

Sift:

2 cups flour
¼ tsp. salt
½ tsp. baking powder
½ tsp. baking soda

Cream until light:

¼ cup margarine
¾ cup brown sugar or **1 cup white sugar**

Then beat in:

1 cup mashed bananas (about 3)

Alternate adding the wet mixture to the flour mixture in about 3 parts with:

3 Tbsp. water or **soymilk**
1 tsp. vanilla

Stir until blended only.

Fold in ½ **cup chopped nuts** (opt.). Pour batter into an oiled loaf pan. Bake at 350° for 1 hour.

CAROL'S VANILLA COOKIES
Makes 2½ dozen

⅓ cup margarine   2 tsp. vanilla
1 cup sugar   2 cups flour
¼ cup soymilk   2 tsp. baking powder
   or water   ½ tsp. salt

Cream margarine and sugar, then add the soymilk and vanilla.

Sift dry ingredients together and gradually add to margarine-sugar mix. Flour hands and make 1" balls of dough. Put on oiled cookie sheet about 1½-2" apart. Bake at 350° for 8-10 minutes or until golden brown on bottom and edges.

CHOCOLATE CHIP COOKIES
Makes 4 dozen

2½ cups flour
1½ tsp. baking powder
½ tsp. salt   6 Tbsp. water
½ cup brown sugar   ½ tsp. vanilla
½ cup white sugar   ½ cup chocolate
½ cup margarine   chips

Sift flour, baking powder, and salt. Cream sugars and margarine. Add water and vanilla and beat till blended. Add dry ingredients to creamed mixture and mix well. Add chocolate chips, mix well. Drop by teaspoons on oiled cookie sheets. Bake at 350° for 15 minutes or until golden on the bottom.

SORGHUM COOKIES

Heat until liquid:
  1-1½ cups sorghum molasses
  3 Tbsp. oil
Add:
  3 Tbsp. grated lemon or **orange rind**
  ½ tsp. ground cardamom
  ¼ tsp. ground cloves
  2 tsp. cinnamon
Sift into mixture:
  3½ cups whole wheat flour
  1 Tbsp. baking powder

Mix into a stiff dough. Drop by spoonfuls onto oiled cookie sheet and flatten with a fork. Bake 20-25 minutes at 350°. Overbaking makes very hard cookies.

PEANUT BUTTER COOKIES

Cream together: Sift and add:
  1 cup peanut butter 2 cups flour
  ½ cup margarine   ½ tsp. salt
  1 cup honey   2 tsp. baking powder
  ½ tsp. vanilla

Roll into little balls. Place on an oiled cookie sheet and flatten with a fork which has been dipped in oil or water.

Bake at 375° for 15 minutes.

OATMEAL COOKIES
Makes about 5 dozen

½ **cup margarine**
⅓ **cup oil**
1 cup brown sugar, packed
1 cup white sugar
⅓ **cup soymilk**
2 tsp. vanilla
2½ cups flour
1 tsp. baking powder
1 tsp. baking soda
1 tsp. salt
3 cups rolled oats
½ **cup raisins** (opt.)

Cream margarine and oil together, then cream in the sugars. Add soymilk and vanilla. Beat until smooth. Beat in flour, baking powder, soda and salt. Mix, add oats and raisins and blend in well. Bake at 350° for about 15 minutes or until the undersides just start turning brown.

NUTRITION NOTES

Vegetarian nutrition is pretty similar to conventional nutrition except in the special areas of protein, vitamin B12, and the feeding of small children. Most nutrients come from standard sources: vitamin A from dark green vegetables, yellow root vegetables, some yellow fruits, and fortified margarine; vitamin C from dark leafy greens and citrus (also potatoes, cauliflower, sweet potatoes, and broccoli). Iron is abundant in legumes and greens; calcium in grains, greens, and soybeans; and the B vitamins in whole grains, potatoes, nutritional yeast, fortified breads and flours, and many fresh vegetables.

Soybeans are a very important food, supplying protein, iron, B vitamins, and calcium.

Protein for Complete Vegetarians

The word *protein* comes from the Greek word *proteios* which means *primary.* You are mostly made of protein except for water and the mineral portions of bones. It forms the muscles and skin, hair and nails, the hemoglobin of the blood which carries oxygen to the body; it forms enzymes and most hormones which regulate the metabolism and functions of the body; it helps maintain the fluid balance of the body and acts as a buffer for acid and base; and it forms the antibodies which protect you from unfriendly microorganisms.

Protein is made up of smaller units called amino acids. There are 22 amino acids. In different combinations and different numbers, they make up the different proteins of the body. Fats, carbohydrates and proteins are all made of carbon, oxygen and hydrogen, but protein contains the added element of nitrogen (and sometimes sulfur). Your body can synthesize most of the amino acids. These are called the *non-essential amino acids.* The amino acids which cannot be synthesized by the body from nitrogen and other substances containing carbon, oxygen and hydrogen are called *essential amino acids.* There are eight of them: tryptophan, threonine, isoleucine, leucine, lysine, methionine, phenylalanine, and valine. A ninth, histidine, is essential to babies for growth.

The body's own protein is constantly being broken down into amino acids and resynthesized back into proteins. These amino acids are not different from those obtained from food. Together they form the amino acid pool that services the body. Some nitrogen is always being excreted and some is always being added by eating. New amino acids are needed to replace those already present and to form new protein for growth and healing. If the nitrogen lost is the same amount as the nitrogen gained, the body is in "nitrogen balance." Growing children and pregnant and nursing ladies should be in "positive nitrogen balance"—that is, more gained than lost.

The function of protein is mainly to provide for tissue growth and repair, but if the carbohydrate and fat intake (calories) is inadequate, it will be used for fuel. Carbohydrates and fats are called "protein-sparing" because they leave the protein for its own special functions.

When you eat the protein of plants, which they make from the nitrogen of the soil and air, it's absorbed as amino acids and resynthesized as protein in the tissues. To resynthesize in the tissues, the essential amino acids need to be in a specific ratio. If an essential amino acid is missing, the other essential amino acids that would make up the complete protein in the tissues are unusable as such and are broken down into fats or sugars (certain ones go to fat and certain ones to sugar), and the nitrogen is lost as urea or goes to form non-essential amino acids. If a certain amino acid is lower in proportion to the others than it should be, the protein will resynthesize in the tissues up to the level of the *limiting amino acid* (or acids) and the remaining ones that are incomplete will break down.

Vegetable Sources of High Quality Proteins

Soybeans and soy products such as soymilk, tofu, yogurt, and tempeh have within them a *complete* protein. All the essential amino acids are present and in the right proportions, and their protein is as growth-promoting as that of meat or dairy products.

There is also high quality protein in wheat germ, oats, garbanzo beans, sunflower seeds, buckwheat (kasha), red, white and black beans, rice, peanuts, pumpkin seeds and cashews. These are foods whose *limiting amino acid* reaches at least 70% of that of an *ideal protein.* * In other words, 70% of the protein within the food is complete. The remainder of the protein can be made complete by combining the food with another food which is high in the limiting amino acid.

In plants, the usual limiting essential amino acids are lysine, methionine, and tryptophan. (Since another amino acid called cystine can be converted to methionine, these two can be grouped together as the "sulfur-containing amino acids," or S.C.) The limiting amino acid in grains, seeds, and nuts is lysine. The sulfur-containing amino acids are limiting in beans. Tryptophan is limiting in some grains and in some beans.

So, when combining plant proteins for optimum quality, the basic combination is beans served with grains, nuts or seeds. Grains also combine well with nutritional yeast. Soybeans and soy products do not need to be combined as they are complete in themselves. But soymilk or a little tofu added to any meal will boost its protein quality and quantity.

There is also high quality protein in many fresh vegetables. But the quantity of protein is not high like grains or beans. However, if large amounts of the following vegetables are eaten, they can contribute substantially to the protein requirements: green beans, swiss chard, broccoli, mustard greens, asparagus, and potatoes.

*Amino Acid Pattern for High Quality Proteins in *Recommended Dietary Allowances,* 8th Revised Edition. Food and Nutrition Board, National Research Council. National Academy of Sciences, Washington, D.C. 1974, page 4.

A WORD

If you are a complete vegetarian, eating only plant food, you will need to supplement vitamin B12. This vitamin does not occur in the vegetable kingdom, and a lack of it can cause severe nervous system damage. The basic source of B12 in nature is synthesis by micro-organisms. (It is synthesized by intestinal flora but most people are unable to absorb it because it is produced in a lower part of the intestine than where it must be absorbed.)

Crystalline B12 is obtained from synthesis by *Streptomyces griseus* (the micro-organism that produces *streptomycin*). Some brands of nutritional yeast and TVP contain added B12. It does not occur naturally in yeast or yogurt. A tiny bit of B12 is produced by the bacteria that ferment miso. But you would have to eat 2 cups of miso a day to get 1 mcg. of B12.

In a large community you can add crystalline B12 to a mass-produced staple food that everyone eats, such as soymilk. In a small community or family, it is more practical to take a 25 mcg. tab twice a week. The body stores extra B12 in the liver (the only B vitamin stored for more than days or weeks), but only absorbs a few micrograms at a time. You cannot get too much, but if you take a lot at a time orally, it won't all get absorbed.

If you use dairy products, ignore this whole page.

about
B12

Prenatal Nutrition

While you're pregnant, you will need a well-rounded diet with about 30% more protein and vitamins than before you were pregnant. You will need to eat lots of fresh vegetables, especially dark leafy greens. Although your metabolism increases during pregnancy, you don't need to increase your calories too much, because pregnant women are somewhat less active than non-pregnant women, and it comes out about even. An increase of about 200-300 calories a day, mostly in the latter half of pregnancy, will suffice.

You should drink a lot—about three quarts of liquid a day. This will help you avoid constipation and keep your body flushed out, since your body is working harder than usual growing a baby.

Supplementary Vitamins and Minerals—It is a good idea to take prenatal vitamins and minerals to make good and sure there are enough vitamins and minerals for both you and the baby. Building a baby from the ground up and nourishing the baby day by day increases your need for these nutrients. Even if you conscientiously try to eat all your dark leafy greens and grains and nutritional yeast, it feels good to be sure. Prenatal vitamins differ from regular multi-vitamins in that they contain extra amounts of all the vitamins and minerals that you need for both of you, and a generous amount of iron. Speaking of iron . . .

Iron—You should take one to three iron pills a day (ferrous sulfate or ferrous gluconate, 5 grains) depending on your iron-level blood tests. If your blood is not checked for iron regularly, you should take one tablet three times a day (three tablets). If you take iron with meals, it is easier on your stomach.

Calcium—Pregnant ladies in their last half of pregnancy, and nursing mothers, need to add about 1 gram (15 grains) of calcium carbonate, calcium gluconate or dicalcium phosphate to their diet each day. The most readily absorbed form of calcium is calcium carbonate, next is calcium gluconate. If you take calcium lactate, you will need about twice as much—2 grams.

Protein—You can get plenty of protein in your pregnancy by eating daily a cup of soybeans and drinking a cup and a half of soymilk or soy yogurt, or by eating half a pound (about a cup) of tofu and drinking a pint of soymilk or soy yogurt, or by eating a cup of hydrated TVP and drinking a quart of soymilk or soy yogurt, or by drinking a quart of soymilk or soy yogurt and eating half a cup of soybeans. If you eat dairy products as well, you should get enough protein from eating daily two cups of cottage cheese, or drinking a quart of milk, yogurt, or buttermilk and eating half a cup of cottage cheese. If you have a little morning sickness, try soy yogurt, soymilk and tofu. They are very mild on the stomach.

Other protein foods include beans and grains eaten together and peanut butter sandwiches.

FEEDING YOUR BABY

Breast Milk—When you are fully nursing with no solid supplement, you give your baby about 800-1000 ml. of milk a day (about one quart). This milk provides everything baby needs for the first 6-8 months if you are well-nourished yourself. You should continue taking pre-natal vitamins and 1 gram of calcium daily throughout nursing to make sure there are plenty of vitamins and minerals for you and your milk.

Breastmilk is very healthful for baby because it contains white blood cells, antibodies, and other substances which destroy germs.

Formula—If you must give baby a formula, look on the labels and find a brand that contains 1.5% protein (with 60% lactalbumin and 40% casein), 7% carbohydrate (lactose), and is fortified with iron and vitamin D. Never give a young baby straight cow's milk or straight soymilk,  because it contains too much protein for baby's system to handle.

If you need to give a bottle because you are working, you could consider pumping or hand-expressing some of your milk to be refrigerated and given while you are away.

Vitamin D—The best source of vitamin D is sunlight. Sunlight reacts with oils in the skin to form vitamin D. If you live in a relatively sunless situation such as a northern or cloudy country or a city with a lot of pollution, you will need to supplement vitamin D. You can give vitamin drops which contain vitamins D, A and C. Vitamin D is important for preventing rickets, a condition found in northern or cloudy countries or in children in big city tenements who don't see the sun. Rickets is not found in the more tropical latitudes except in unusual circumstances, such as totally occlusive clothing.

Vitamin D is stored in the body, so a lot of sun on the skin in the summer can last through the winter.

Food—It is best to avoid supplemental feeding for the first 4 months. Baby's digestive system cannot always handle foreign protein or complex starches before this time. Your milk has all the nutrients baby needs for the first 6-8 months, *with the exception of vitamin D.*

If you want to feed baby before 4 months, give only processed baby pablum and/or applesauce. If given too early, proteins and some fruits such as oranges and strawberries can cause food intolerance. **Also, keep in mind that the more food you feed, the less breastmilk is consumed, and therefore less high-quality milk nutrients are consumed.**

Strained Fruits, Vegetables, and Processed Pablum can be introduced at 4-6 months. (But you don't need to until 6-8 months if you don't want to.) Introduce one food at a time and wait several days to see how it is tolerated. Start with applesauce and bananas and rice cereal. Gradually introduce other strained fruits and vegetables. Don't give orange juice until 6 months and don't give strawberries until one year.

Starches and Unprocessed Grains can be introduced at 6-8 months. Mashed cooked grains are different from processed baby cereal (pablum) and are harder to digest.

Thin the strained rice or potatoes with extra liquid at first. For oatmeal, use the instant de-hulled kind. At 6-8 months, babies like to gum toast, cookies, or crackers. Watch them carefully when they start eating these foods until they learn to gum, chew and swallow right. Plain bread is not as good as toast because babies can choke on it until they really have the hang of it. So begin on toast and teething cookies.

Soymilk, Soymilk Yogurt, and Tofu (Bean Curd) can be introduced at 7-8 months. Sterilize the soymilk as you would cow's milk until baby is a year old. You can give your baby soymilk yogurt at this age, too.

Tofu is a good milk protein food for baby. Blend it up or put it through a strainer until he can gum the soft curd un-assisted. Tofu is twice as concentrated in protein and other nutrients as soymilk. Give lots of water when you start soymilk or soymilk products (or whole cow's milk).

Nutritional Yeast can be sprinkled on baby's food after 8 months. It is an excellent source of B vitamins, and most brands add B12.

Legumes—You can start trying baby out on beans at 8-9 months. Thin split pea soup is a good one to start with. Any beans you feed your baby must be cooked until *very* soft, skinned, and put through a sieve, blender, or baby food grinder. Add liquid to the mashed beans to make them a soupy consistency rather than a thick paste. Try one kind of bean at a time so you can see which agrees. You can tell whether or not baby is digesting his beans by checking his poop. If the beans come through mostly unchanged or if it smells sour, they aren't being digested. If this happens, stop the beans and give your baby breastmilk, yogurt, and a bland diet for a day or so. Try the beans again now and then, but it is okay if baby can't handle them for a while. You can try soybeans, but they must be *very, very soft,* skinned (remove skins after cooking, or rub the uncooked beans together under water till the skins all come off), and mashed or sieved till smooth. If they are at all crunchy, they will cause diarrhea and a sore red bottom. If they are well-cooked, soybeans do well with most babies. Be sure to add some liquid to the strained or blended soybeans, and be sure to skin them until baby tolerates them really well. Then you can mash them with the skins on.

If baby cannot handle soybeans, don't worry. Some children can't eat them until they are 2-3 years old. The soymilk products and/or "high-protein" baby cereal can cover a child's protein needs indefinitely. High-protein cereal contains enough protein in 1½ cups to meet a child's daily protein requirement through age 3.

Vitamin B12—Baby will get vitamin B12 from your milk as long as he is nursing a lot. Make sure you have a good source of B12 so your milk has it. Your prenatal vitamins probably contain plenty. When baby is weaned or weaning, he will need to be supplemented with B12 just like vegetarian children and adults.

> *Don't give baby honey before one year of age. There is evidence that honey can contain botulism spores.*

Water—If baby is totally breastfed and you nurse often, additional water isn't necessary. If you give a formula and/or additional food, you must give baby lots of water. Sterilize water until baby is 9-12 months old.

*Reported by the Bacterial Diseases Division, Bureau of Epidemiology, Center for Disease Control.

Feeding Your Young Vegetarian Child

Usually, by one year of age, your child is eating most grown-up food, chopped finely, three meals a day plus snacks. The main nutrient you need to be aware of for the vegetarian child is protein. Soybeans and soy products are the main protein source in the Farm's high-protein vegetarian diet, and these foods need to be steadily worked into your toddler's diet.

Most children can handle soy--milk, soymilk yogurt, and tofu (bean curd) by the time they are 7-8 months old, and de-skinned (either remove skins after cooking, rub skins off under hot water before cooking, or strain through a fine sieve), mashed or blendered soybeans by 8-10 months. If your child can handle it, he should be given soy products every day—a glass of soymilk, raw or lightly cooked tofu, mashed soybeans in a bowl, soy yogurt, soyburgers, or mashed soybeans rolled up in a soft tortilla (our kids' favorite).

The Recommended Daily Allowance for protein for 1-3 year olds is 24 grams a day. About ⅔ of this should come from soy. The remaining ⅓ will come from combinations of grains and vegetables in the rest of the diet. One cup of whole soybeans, or ⅔ cup of mashed soybeans, contains 22 grams of protein.

There are some children who can tolerate soymilk products but not soybeans themselves. They will outgrow this in time, usually by 2-2½ years. Meanwhile, there are other sources of protein. If your child can handle the soymilk products but not the beans, 3 cups of soymilk a day will give 24 grams of protein. Yogurt is the same, and tofu is twice as concentrated as soymilk, so half the amount would provide the recommended daily requirement. If you give him soybeans or some of these soymilk products every day, and a balanced variety of grains, vegetables and fruits, he will be very well nourished.

If your child cannot handle soymilk, try soymilk yogurt and tofu. If they don't work either, give her "high protein" baby cereal (the commercially packaged kind). The soy in this cereal has been processed so that it is very easily digested. 1½ cups of the dry high-protein cereal will provide 20 grams of protein.

You can also make the *High-Protein Soy Bread* on page 174. This bread will have about 7 grams of protein per slice and makes excellent sandwiches or toast.

Peanut butter sandwiches are also a good source of protein for toddlers. It is important to eat the peanut butter with a grain such as bread or crackers because peanuts (or beans) eaten with grains each make the protein of the other more complete and usable.

Other legumes are a good source of protein when eaten with a grain at the same meal. Three-fourths cup of pinto bean or kidney bean chili with two slices of bread will provide about 17 grams of protein (24 grams if you use soy bread). There is a little protein in most vegetables, breads, root vegetables,  etc. So, a well-rounded diet with soy (or soy cereal) as its center will provide quite a bit of protein when you count it up.

If your young child doesn't eat well, try feeding him with other children with good appetites. Don't force him. If you don't feel a kid is eating enough vegetables for vitamins, give chewable kid vitamins until tastes change and mature—they will. Some vegetarian children are anemic (as are many other children) because they don't eat enough beans, iron-containing vegetables, or iron-fortified cereals. If your child is a picky eater and seems pale, tired, and/or irritable, check his blood hematocrit (especially if he is between 9 and 24 months old). This test for anemia is a good check on his nutritional state. If he is anemic, give him kid vitamins with iron.

And don't forget the value of the potato. If eaten in quantity (and most children really like it), the potato has lots of B vitamins and a good amount of vitamin C, as well as minerals and the calories children need. If there are many hours between meals, give your child snacks such as soymilk, raw vegetables, fruit, cookies, or crackers.

Vitamin D

If you live in a northern latitude or in a sunless or cloudy situation, you will need to give your child a vitamin D supplement or a multivitamin containing 400 IU of vitamin D. If you live in a southern latitude, and your child's skin is exposed to the sun, the oils in the skin will react with the sunlight and synthesize vitamin D.

Vitamin B12

If you are feeding your child a totally vegetarian diet— that is, no dairy products or eggs—you will need to give a B12 supplement. You can use a commercial food yeast which has already been fortified with B12, or any other prepared food that is already supplemented (check labels). If you don't use a fortified food, give your child a 10 mcg. or a 25 mcg. (sometimes 10's aren't available) tab of B12, crushed in food, three times a week.

INDEX

INDEX

For help with your vegetarian diet or large-quantity vegetarian cooking, or finding ingredients for any of the recipes in this book, write to: The Book Publishing Co., Dept. F, 156 Drakes Lane, Summertown, Tennessee 38483.

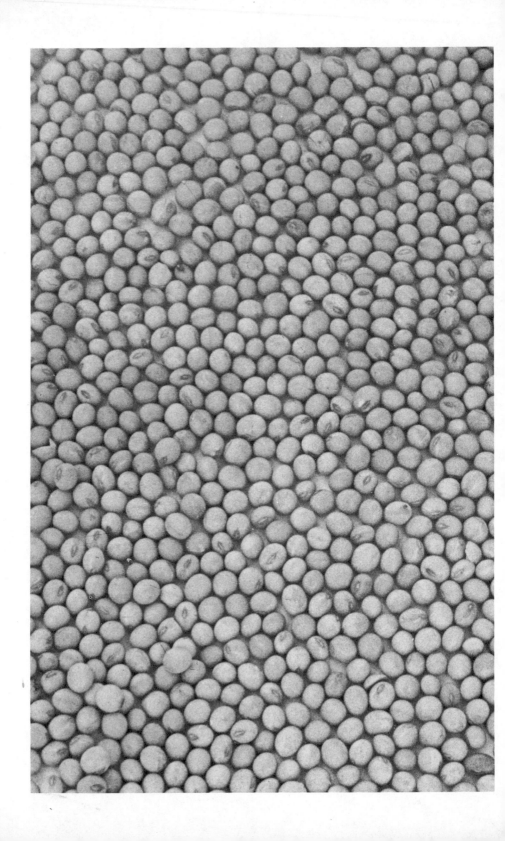